LEAVES FROM THE TREE OF LIFE

Sermons for Children on the Truths about Jesus that Heal the Soul

RICHARD NEWTON

SOLID GROUND CHRISTIAN BOOKS
Birmingham, Alabama USA
February 2011

OTHER RELATED TITLES FOR CHILDREN

In addition to *Leaves from the Tree of Life* we are delighted to offer several other titles from Solid Ground Christian Books for the young. Here is a sample:

Little Pillows and Morning Bells by Miss Havergal
Morning Stars by Miss Havergal
The Child's Book on the Fall by Thomas H Gallaudet
The Child's Book on the Soul by T.H. Gallaudet
The Child's Book of Natural Theology by Gallaudet
The Child's Book on the Sabbath by Horace Hooker
Feed My Lambs by John Todd
Truth Made Simple by John Todd
The Tract Primer by the American Tract Society
The Child at Home by John S.C. Abbott
Early Piety Illustrated by Gorham Abbott
Repentance & Faith for the Young by Charles Walker
Jesus the Way by Edward Payson Hammond
The Pastor's Daughter by Louisa Payson Hopkins
Lectures on the Bible to the Young by John Eadie
The Scripture Guide by James W. Alexander
My Brother's Keeper by James W. Alexander
The Chief End of Man by John Hall
Old Paths for Little Feet by Carol Brandt
Small Talks on Big Questions by Selah Helms
Advice to a Young Christian by Jared Waterbury
Bible Promises by Richard Newton
Bible Warnings by Richard Newton
Bible Models by Richard Newton
Bible Animals by Richard Newton
Bible Jewels by Richard Newton
Heroes of the Early Church by Richard Newton
Heroes of the Reformation by Richard Newton
Safe Compass and How it Points by Richard Newton
The King's Highway by Richard Newton
The Life of Jesus Christ for the Young by Richard Newton
Rays from the Sun of Righteousness by Richard Newton

Call us at **1-205-443-0311**
Visit us on-line at www.solid-ground-books.com

LEAVES

FROM

THE TREE OF LIFE

BY THE

Rev. RICHARD NEWTON, D.D.
AUTHOR OF
'BIBLE WONDERS' 'NATURE'S WONDERS' 'BIBLE BLESSINGS'
'BEST THINGS' ETC.

EDINBURGH
W. P. NIMMO, HAY, & MITCHELL

Solid Ground Christian Books
PO Box 660132
Vestavia Hills AL 35266
205-443-0311
sgcb@charter.net
www.solid-ground-books.com

LEAVES FROM THE TREE OF LIFE
Sermons to Children on the Truths about Jesus that Heal the Soul

by Richard Newton (1813-1887)

Taken from the 1882 edition by *Nimmo, Hay & Mitchell, Edinburgh*

Cover image is taken from a photo by Ric Ergenbright
Huckleberry leaves, McKenzie Pass, Oregon Cascades Range

Cover design by Borgo Design
Contact them at borgogirl@bellsouth.net

ISBN- 978-159925-150-9

PREFACE.

THIS book has much to say about healing. And to souls diseased by sin, as ours are, this is a matter of the greatest importance. We see its importance when we remember that one of the sweet names by which our blessed Saviour is spoken of in the Old Testament is 'Jehovah-Rophi,' or 'The Lord who *healeth*.'

The chief means that He makes use of in healing souls is the truth about Jesus, of which the Bible tells us. 'He sent His *word*, and *healed* them,' says David.

This little book, in the truths of which it tells, is like a branch from the Tree of Life full of leaves. They are all *healing* leaves. But it is not by any power of their own that they are able to heal. They can only do this as God blesses them. If any of the readers of this book desire that it shall do them good, they must ask God to give it healing power, and bless it to their souls.

It is more than twenty years ago since the writer of

this book first engaged in the work of preaching to children, and making books of the sermons. He was first led to do this by thinking on the words of Jesus to Peter, 'Lovest Thou me? *Feed my lambs.*' This is the twelfth volume he has been permitted to publish. He has been encouraged to go on in this work by many cheering testimonies to the usefulness of these books, received from various parts of America, as well as from other lands. In answer to these testimonies, this new volume is now sent forth as an expression of the writer's cordial love to the lambs of Jesus everywhere. The hope of affording any help to them in trying to love and serve Jesus, is one of the sweetest comforts of his life. And the earnest prayer of his heart is, that it may please God to bless this book, and make it a blessing to all who read its pages.

CONTENTS.

		PAGE
I.	THE BIBLE COMPARED TO A TREE OF LIFE,	7
II.	THE LESSON OF OBEDIENCE,	22
III.	THE LEAF FOR CURING LYING,	36
IV.	THE LEAF FOR HEALING COVETOUSNESS,	49
V.	THE LESSON OF PATIENCE,	63
VI.	THE LEAF FOR HEALING IDLENESS,	79
VII.	THE LEAF FOR CURING PRIDE,	94
VIII.	THE LEAF FOR HEALING THE EVIL CONSCIENCE,	111
IX.	THE LEAF FOR CURING QUARRELS,	128
X.	THE LESSON OF FAITHFULNESS,	144

LEAVES FROM THE TREE OF LIFE.

I.

'𝔄nd the leaves of the tree were for the healing of the nations.'—
REV. xxii. 2.

THIS verse carries us up to heaven. That blessed place is described in this chapter as a city, called the New Jerusalem. This city is spoken of as being very beautiful. Nothing like it was ever seen in this world. It had walls of jasper, and foundations of precious stones. Its streets were paved with gold; but the gold there was different from any we have ever seen. It was so clear that you might see through it, just as you see through glass. It had twelve gates, and every gate was made of one great pearl.

This is the home which Jesus is preparing for His people. If we love and serve Him, He will take us to this glorious home at last. What a blessed thing it will be to have such a home as this! And what a joy and delight it will be to meet with many we have known and loved, and all the good people who will be found there!

But the apostle tells us more about this heavenly city which he saw. He says there was a river of water, clear as crystal, running through the midst of the city; and on either side of the river there was the tree of life. This tree bore twelve different kinds of fruit. It yielded its fruit every month ; '*and the leaves of the tree were for the healing of the nations.*'

What a wonderful tree this must be! There was something like this in the garden of Eden, where God put Adam and Eve when they were created. Some people think that, even if Adam and Eve had not sinned, their bodies would have been liable to grow old and decay, and that the tree of life had power to prevent this. They suppose that God put that tree of life in the garden on purpose that our first parents might eat of its fruit, and in that way be able to live for ever.

I think this was very likely; for when God sent Adam and Eve out of the garden, after they had sinned, He did it for this very reason, '*lest they should eat of the tree of life, and live for ever.*' I suppose that the tree of life which was in the garden of Eden was a tree which had the power to keep the bodies of those who ate of it from decaying and dying. And in that heavenly city, where those who love Jesus will live with Him, we are told there will be a tree of life like that which was in the garden of Eden. And this is the tree spoken of in our text, where it says, 'And the leaves of the tree were for the healing of the nations.'

This is a hard text to explain. If you ask me what it means, I know not that I can tell you in such a way that you can understand it, but I will try.

I think the leaves of this tree are not intended for the use of those who are in heaven, but for those who are not in heaven.

There are two reasons for this: one is, that when we get to heaven, we shall be so happy and perfect that we shall need no healing. There will be nothing left in us to heal. And, of course, if we have nothing to heal, we shall not need leaves from the tree of life to heal us. This is plain enough. We can all understand this.

And the other reason why I think these leaves cannot be intended for the use of those who are in heaven is, that it says they are 'for the healing of the *nations.*' But there will be no *nations* in heaven. There will be some people there, no doubt, out of all nations, but the nations themselves will not be there. The English nation will not be in heaven, but a great many good English people will be there. The American nation will not be there, but a great many good American people will be there. And if those who live in heaven need no healing, and if there will be no nations in heaven, then it is certain that these 'leaves from the tree of life' are intended for the use of persons outside of heaven.

And if the nations healed by the leaves of the tree of life are not people in heaven, then who are meant by them? Listen, while I give you the best answer I can to this question.

The Bible teaches us, you know, that when Jesus comes back again to our earth the resurrection will take place. He will raise from their graves the bodies of all His people who have died from the beginning of the world. Those of His people who shall be living when He comes He will change. In a moment, in the twinkling of an eye, they will be made as beautiful and as glorious as Jesus looked when He was on the Mount of Transfiguration. Then Jesus will take all His people away with Him to live in that beautiful city which the apostle tells us about in the last two chapters of the New Testament.

After this, many good people think that Jesus will change our earth, and purify it by fire, and make it beautiful as the garden of Eden was. And they think that those left in the world then will be made up of different nations, just as it is now, only, as

Isaiah says, 'The people will be all righteous.' They will all love and serve Jesus, and the whole world will be full of peace, and joy, and happiness. And the people who will then be living in the world, it is supposed, are 'the nations' who will need the leaves from the tree of life to keep their bodies from getting sick and dying.

And it is thought that the people of Jesus, living with Him in that heavenly city, will often go backwards and forwards from heaven to earth, just as the angels do now. They will gather the leaves from the tree of life in the heavenly city, and bring them down to this world, and distribute them for the healing of the nations who will then be living here.

I do not say certainly that this is the meaning of the text; but it is the best account of it that I can give. If anybody will give me a better account of what this text means, I shall feel very much obliged to him.

But this is not what I am going to talk about. I wish to speak of plain, simple things; things in this world in which we live, and things that we can all understand.

We know that there *are nations* living here now, and we know that these nations do need healing. Both their bodies and their souls need healing. But where is the tree of life whose leaves are for the healing of these nations? Oh, if there only were a real tree of this kind,—a tree whose leaves could heal the souls of men of all the diseases which sin has brought upon them,—what a blessed thing it would be to be occupied all the time in gathering the leaves from this tree, and in carrying them round to heal the souls that were sick and make them well! Why, if I had a hundred lives, I should want to spend them all in just this kind of work. But we have no such tree. Yet we have *something like it.* We have something that may be *compared* to a tree of life. This is the Bible. Solomon says, Proverbs iii. 18, that wisdom, or the religion which the Bible teaches, is '*a tree of life* to them who lay hold on her.' We may well compare the Bible, therefore, to a tree of life. And when we think of it as such a tree, then the verses from the Bible, which we take as our texts to preach from, are just like leaves from the tree of life. This is the way in which God wants us to use the Bible; and this is what David means, in speaking of God's dealings with the Israelites, when he says, 'He sent His *word*, and *healed* them' (Psalm cvii. 20).

'*The leaves of the tree were for the healing of the nations.*'

I have taken these words for our text, in beginning a new course of Children's Sermons, because I wish to show how God makes use of the Bible to change our wicked hearts and tempers, and make us like Jesus. When doing this, God is healing our souls. And when we take one text of Scripture after another, and try to show how each is intended to help us in overcoming some sin, or correcting something that is wrong in our hearts and lives, it will be like taking leaves from the tree of life and using them to heal the diseases of our souls.

Our sermon to-day is about—*The Bible as a tree of life.*

I wish to speak of *three* reasons why it may be thus spoken of.

In the first place, the Bible is like a tree of life because IT GIVES LIFE TO DEAD SOULS.

A dead soul! What is a dead soul? It is a soul that does not love God, or think about Him, or try to serve Him. Suppose you find the body of a man lying in a field. You look at it. You wish to know whether it is alive or dead. You put your hand on it, and find that it is warm. You watch it, and see that it breathes. You strike it, and it flinches, thus showing that it feels. You raise it up, and find that it can move. Is that body dead or alive? It is alive. But suppose when you lift it up it falls down again like a log. Suppose you strike it, and it has no more feeling than a stone. You lay your hand upon it, and find it cold as marble. You watch it, but it does not breathe. What then? Is it alive or dead? It is dead. This is the way to tell whether a *body* is alive or dead. And it is just the same with the soul. The Bible tells us that before we become Christians we are all 'dead in trespasses and sins.' This means that our souls are dead. And you can tell whether a soul is dead or not, just as you tell whether a body is dead.

Dead souls do not breathe. Prayer is the breath of the soul; but dead souls do not pray. Dead souls are cold. Love to God is what warms the soul; but unconverted people do not love God. Their souls are cold because they are dead. Dead souls have no feeling. A live soul shows its feeling by hating sin, and trying to get rid of it; but unconverted people do not hate sin, or try to get rid of it. Their souls have no feeling. Dead souls do not move. Serving God, trying to please Him and reach heaven, are the ways in which live souls move; but unconverted people do not serve God, they do not try to please Him and get to heaven. Their souls are dead; they have no motion. A soul that does not breathe, or feel, that is cold, and has no motion, is a dead soul.

And the most important thing in the world to be done for a dead soul is to give it life. This is what the Bible calls conversion, or 'being born again.' And the Bible may well be called a 'tree of life,' because this is just what it does. It gives life to dead souls; it converts them. And when we teach or preach what the Bible tells about Jesus, then we are taking leaves from the tree of life and using them to heal dead souls, or give them life.

Where there is no Bible there is no tree of life, and so people are not converted there. But where the Bible is taught or preached, there the tree of life is growing, and dead souls are healed, or made alive.

When the Apostle Peter began to preach the gospel on the day of Pentecost, he preached a very plain, simple sermon. But it was all about Jesus, and what He has done for us; yet three thousand dead souls were made alive by that one sermon. Oh, it just seems to me as if Peter had gone and filled his arms with branches from the tree of life, and then, standing among the crowd of people around him, had plucked the leaves from the branches and scattered them about, and wherever one of those leaves fell, it gave life to some dead soul!

And there is no book but the Bible that will convert people, or make dead souls alive. Suppose we go into a village in some destitute part of the country. There is no church or Sunday-school there. The souls of the people are dead; there are no conversions.

You may open a week-day school, and teach the children to read and to write. You may teach them arithmetic, and geography, and history, and philosophy. This may make those children bright and intelligent, but it will not convert them; it will not give life to their dead souls. But suppose a Sunday-school missionary goes there. He opens a school. He gathers the children. He reads the Bible, and teaches them about Jesus. He 'tells them the old, old story, of Jesus and His love.'

And as he does this, some of them are led to feel that they are sinners. They begin to pray. Their hearts are changed. They are converted. They learn to love Jesus, and serve Him. Their souls that were dead are made alive. The Sunday-school missionary brought leaves from the tree of life, and their souls are healed. This is what the Bible does all the time. It may well be called the tree of life, because it gives life to dead souls.

The Bible may be called the tree of life, in the second place, because IT PRESERVES LIFE, *as well as gives it.*

Are our bodies able to keep themselves alive? No. If they are deprived of food, what will become of them? They will die. Our bodies need *food*, then, to keep them alive. And this is the reason why Jesus put these words, in that beautiful prayer which He has left us to teach us how to pray: 'Give us this day our daily bread.' Bread here means food, such food as we need to preserve the life of our bodies.

And our souls cannot live without food, any more than our bodies can. And as it is only 'leaves from the tree of life,' or what the Bible tells about Jesus, that can *give life* to dead souls, so it is only 'leaves from the tree of life,' or what the Bible tells about Jesus, that can *keep our souls alive.*

When the children of Israel were going through the wilderness, God fed them with manna. This fell round their tents every night, like a light fall of snow, or, as the Bible says, 'like hoar-frost.' And this is what David means when he says that God 'sent them bread from heaven.' They lived on this. It was the food which preserved the life of their bodies.

And the truth of the Bible, or the things which it tells us about Jesus, is sometimes called *manna*, sometimes *bread*, or *milk*, or *wine*, or *meat;* because it is the food of the soul, or that by which its life is preserved. And nothing but the Bible can keep our souls alive.

THE BIBLE A TREE OF LIFE.

Many persons think that unless they go to church, and hear sermons, and take the Lord's Supper, their souls cannot live or grow in grace. This is a mistake.

Going to church and hearing sermons are very useful things. They are great helps in trying to serve God, as Christian people ought to do. God gave us these blessings because He knew how useful they would be. But then these things are not absolutely necessary. If we only have the Bible, and make a right use of it, it is possible for our souls to live, and serve God, even if we have no churches, or ministers, or sacraments. But this would not be possible without the Bible.

The history of what took place in the island of Madagascar a few years ago shows how true this is.

The missionaries had been preaching there for some years. Schools were opened and churches established. Some parts of the Bible had been translated into the language of the island; and many of the people had become Christians. Then a wicked woman was made queen of the island. She hated the Bible, and the religion which it taught. She resolved to banish the Bible from the island, and restore the worship of the idols to which they had long been accustomed.

So she ordered the missionaries to leave the island; and they were obliged to go. The churches and schools were closed and destroyed. Laws were passed forbidding any person to keep the Bible or to read it. Those who did so, if they were found out, were to be sent to prison or put to death. Then some of the people gave up their Bibles, and went back to the worship of their former idols. But many refused to do this. Some were taken up and cast into prison or put to death; others fled from their homes, and lived in the woods, and in dens and caves of the earth, rather than give up their Bibles. Such portions of the

Bible as they had they kept hid away in secret places, where none but themselves could find them. Then they would meet together by night, or in the woods, to pray, and read the Bible, and talk about it, and encourage each other in the trials they had to bear.

This continued for about twenty years. During that time they never saw a minister, never had either baptism or the Lord's Supper administered to them, and never heard a sermon. They had nothing but a portion of the Bible—a few leaves from the tree of life—to keep their souls alive. Now, under these circumstances, we would think that the Christian people in that island would all have been killed or been forced to give up their Bibles and the religion which caused them so much suffering. We would think that when the missionaries came back to Madagascar they would have found no Christians left, and would have had to begin their work afresh. It was not so, but very different from this; for when the queen died the persecution ceased. Her son, who was made king after her, was favourable to the missionaries, and invited them to come back and open the schools and churches again. Then the persecuted Christians came out from their hiding-places; and, strange as it may seem, their numbers had increased during all those days of cruel persecution. There were many more Christians in that island when the persecution ceased than when it began. The Christians, then, were just like the bush that Moses saw in the wilderness,—it burned with fire, and yet it was not consumed. The Bible kept their souls alive during all those dark and trying days.

The portions of the Bible which they had were like leaves from the tree of life. These healing leaves not only kept alive the souls of those who were Christians, but they also gave life to many whose souls were dead.

The Bible may be compared to a tree of life, in the second place, *because it preserves life* as well as gives it.

The third reason why the Bible may be compared to a tree of life is, because IT MAKES LIFE HAPPY.

God gave us the Bible on purpose that it might be a tree of life to us. He intended that it should *give life* to our souls, that it should *preserve* that life when it was given, and that it should make that life happy. Jesus came into our world on purpose to bless it and make it happy. And those who become real Christians, and make a proper use of the Bible, are the happiest people in the world. The Bible tells us that those who love God ought to be 'merry and joyful.' They have the best reason in the world to be '*always rejoicing,*' and ' in *everything to give thanks.*' And it is easy to see why this is so. For when the Bible makes our souls alive, or leads us to become true Christians, then we know that our sins are all forgiven. This ought to make us happy. We know that Jesus loves us, and is our best friend. This ought to make us happy. And we are sure of going to heaven when we die. Surely there is enough in this to make us happy at all times. And that blessed book which tells us all these good things may well be compared to a tree of life, because it does so much to make us happy.

Now let us look at some examples that show how true it is that the Bible makes people happy.

An aged Christian man was going along once, under a heavy load, on a hot summer's day. He sat down to rest himself by the road-side, under the shadow of a great tree. A person who knew him came along, and stopped to speak with him. As they were talking together, a splendid carriage rolled by. The owner of the carriage—a proud, bad man—was sitting in it, taking his ease.

This friend said to the old man: 'There, do you see that carriage? The man who owns it is a very wicked man. Every one who is acquainted with him knows this. He never goes to church. He hates the Bible and religion. He swears dreadfully, and does a great many wicked things. And yet he is rolling in wealth, and has everything he can wish for. On the other hand, here you are, trying to love and serve God faithfully, and yet see how many trials you have! You can hardly get money enough to buy bread to eat and clothes to put on. Now, if God orders all things about us, and is good and wise, as the Bible teaches, how do you explain it that He often lets wicked people have such an easy time, and allows good people to have such a hard time?'

'Ah,' said the old man, '*it is the end that will explain all.* My road is rough, but it is short, and it leads directly to heaven. That will *make up* for all the difference. I am happier in my poverty, with the hope of heaven, than the wicked man, with all his riches, can be without this hope.'

This is true. The Bible was a tree of life to that poor man, because, in all his poverty and trials, it was making his life happy with the hope of heaven.

But here is another story to show how happy the Bible makes the life of those who believe it and obey it.

One fine summer evening a crowd of workmen were passing along through the streets of the city of Hamburg. As the crowd swept by, an old shoemaker was sitting under a shade before his door, busily engaged in mending a shoe. Sometimes he would stop a little from his work and sing a verse or two of one of the old German psalms, which he loved very much. A well-dressed young man, a student in the University, was going by this evening. When he heard the merry voice of the shoemaker he stopped, and said to him:

'Well, my friend, you seem to be very happy and contented.'

'I *am* happy, sir,' said he; 'and why shouldn't I be?'

'I don't know,' said the student. 'A great many people are not happy. You seem to be very poor. I suppose you have none but yourself to work for?'

'You are mistaken, sir,' said the shoemaker. 'I have a wife and seven children to feed and support with the work of these hands. I'm a poor man, it's true, but that's no reason why I shouldn't work and be happy.'

'I am very much surprised to see a poor workman like you so happy, and I don't understand what can make you so.'

'Stranger,' said the shoemaker, laying down his work, and taking hold of the young man's arm, with a grave and serious look,—'Stranger, I'm not so poor as you think. Let me tell you, *I am a son of the King.*'

The young man turned away, saying to himself, 'Poor fellow, he's crazy! He thinks he's well off when he's poor. This is what makes him happy. I was beginning to think that perhaps he might be able to tell me the great secret I am seeking—the secret of true happiness. But I am mistaken.'

A week went by, and the young student again had occasion to pass the same street. He found the old shoemaker sitting in the same place, still busy with his work, and singing as cheerfully as before. As he passed by, the young man lifted his cap, in a mocking sort of way, and, making a bow to the shoemaker, said, 'Good morning, Mr. Prince.'

'Stop, my friend,' said the shoemaker, laying down his work; 'I wish to say a few words to you, if you please. You left me suddenly the other evening, as if you thought that I was crazy.'

'To tell you the truth,' said the young man, 'that is just what I did think.'

'Well, my friend,' continued the shoemaker, 'I am not crazy. What I said the other evening I said in earnest. It's true, every word of it. *I am a son of the King.* Just sit down here and listen while I tell you about Jesus the King, and the glory of His kingdom.'

Now this young man was a Jew. He had been taught to read the Old Testament Scriptures when he was a child, and to believe in them; but since he had grown up he had given up his faith in the Bible, and had ceased to read it. He was like a sailor out at sea who had lost his compass. He could not tell where he was going, or how to steer, and this made him feel very unhappy. Just as a drowning man will catch at straws, so this young man was ready to catch at anything that seemed likely to aid him in trying to find out how to be happy; so he sat down and listened to his humble friend.

Then the shoemaker began and told him of the promises of the Old Testament about a glorious King, who was to be the Saviour and Ruler of the world. He showed him how all the things that are written in the law of Moses, and in the prophets, and in the Psalms, about this glorious King, had been fulfilled in Jesus Christ. He showed him how He had suffered and died for our sins; how He had risen from the grave, and had gone up to take His seat in glory at the right hand of God. He told him how He had sent His messengers into all the world to tell men of what He had done for them; and how all who repented of their sins, and believed in Him, would be pardoned, and made happy now, and then at last be saved in heaven for ever. He told him how Jesus was going to come back again to this world one of these days, to set up a glorious kingdom; and how all who love and serve Him now will share the glories of that kingdom, and reign with Him for ever.

The young student sat listening with great interest to what his poor friend was saying. He had often read the promises of the Old Testament, but he had never thought of them in connection with Jesus Christ. This was all new to him. He was astonished at what he heard.

'And now, young man,' said the shoemaker, 'don't you see how truly I could say, "I am a son of the King"? Don't you see what reason I have to be contented and happy? It is just because I know Jesus. I believe in Him, and I love Him, and this makes me happy. The Bible tells me that "all things shall work together for good to me;" and that "all things are mine because I am Christ's." Isn't this enough to make any one happy?'

'Where can I learn more about these things?' asked the young man. 'I see that you believe them, and this gives you peace and happiness. But I have no peace, and no happiness. Oh how I long for them!'

Then the shoemaker gave the young man a copy of the Bible. He told him to take it home, and read it carefully, and pray over it, and that he would be sure to find the secret of true happiness there. And he found it. The young Jewish student read the Bible carefully, and found Jesus in it. And in Jesus he found the secret of true happiness. He afterwards became a missionary to his own people, and preached to them about the happiness he had found in Jesus.

And here you see that, when the old shoemaker was giving the Bible to that Jewish student, he was giving him 'leaves from the tree of life,' and those leaves were for the healing of his soul.

And so we have spoken of three reasons why the Bible may be compared to a tree of life. The first reason is, because *it gives life;* the second, because *it preserves life;* the third, because *it makes life happy.*

Let us be thankful that we have this tree of life. Let us make a good use of it ourselves, and do all we can to scatter abroad its leaves 'for the healing of the nations.'

II.

'And He went down with them to Nazareth, and was subject unto them.'—LUKE ii. 51.

THE city of Nazareth is a very interesting place to visit, because it is the place where Jesus lived when he was a boy. We spent a Sunday there while travelling through the Holy Land, and enjoyed the day very much. We had service in one of our tents in the afternoon, and when the service was over, I took a walk through the town, and then up to the top of the hill behind the town, and sat down there to look over the city and country around, and to think such thoughts as would naturally come into one's mind in a place like that. The country about Nazareth is very beautiful. But that which interested me most, as I sat on that hill-top, was not the beauty of the country, but the remembrance of Him who had once lived there. The boy Jesus had lived in that city below me. He had walked over those fields, and played there with other boys. He had climbed the hill that I had just climbed, and possibly had often sat down to rest Himself where I was sitting. I wondered how Jesus played when He was a boy? and what the boys who were his companions thought of Him? I wondered how He talked? and what He said? How He felt? and what He thought about Himself, and about the world that He had come to save? I found it easy to ask myself these questions, but it was not so easy to answer them. *I* could not answer them. Nobody in the world can answer them.

There are a great many things connected with Jesus, when He was a boy, that we know nothing at all about. But the words of our text tell us one thing about Jesus, which is very important, and about which we may be very sure; it is this—Jesus was an *obedient* boy. He went down to Nazareth with His parents, and was subject unto them.

He was twelve years old at the time when this was said of Him. He had been obeying His parents then for twelve years. He kept on obeying them after this for eighteen years longer. Eighteen and twelve make how many? Thirty. Jesus obeyed His parents for thirty years. Some children think that when they get to be eighteen or twenty they are too old to obey, and have a right to do just what they please. But Jesus did not think so. He obeyed His parents till He was twenty-one years of age; and He did not cease then, but went on obeying them for nine years longer.

How wonderful this was! How strange it must have seemed to the angels! They had seen Jesus when He made this world, and the sun and the moon, and all those beautiful worlds around us; and when they saw Him going forth, day after day, to work at the trade of a carpenter, to do just what His father Joseph told Him, and just what His mother Mary wished, how great must have been their astonishment!

When Jesus began His public ministry, He spent a little over three years in it. During those three years He taught the people a great many lessons; but He spent the first *thirty* years of His life in teaching just one lesson—and that is *the lesson of obedience*. And if Jesus spent so much time in teaching this one lesson, then it must be a most important lesson.

We call this little book *Leaves from the Tree of*

Life. This tree of life is the Bible. And the different verses from the Bible that we take as texts, we may consider as leaves from this tree of life. These leaves are intended for the healing of the nations. Every text has power to heal or cure something that is wrong in our hearts or lives. Our present subject is—*The lesson of obedience.*

'*He went down with them to Nazareth, and was subject unto them.*'

If Jesus was willing to spend thirty years of His life to teach this one lesson of obedience, then it is certain that this must be a most important lesson for us to learn. Jesus would not have spent so many years in setting us this example of obedience unless there had been very good reasons for it. There are, indeed, good reasons for it. Let us look at some of these. I wish to speak of three reasons why Jesus set us this example, or three reasons why we should learn to obey.

In the first place, we should learn to obey FOR GOD'S SAKE.

God wants us to do this. We read in the Bible this command: 'Children, obey your parents.' Whose command is this? It is God's command. Then, if we disobey our parents, whom else do we disobey at the same time? God. And so it is when we disobey any other command or law. We disobey God at the same time. God wants us to learn to obey. He tells us in one place in the Bible, 'Submit yourselves to every ordinance of man for the Lord's sake' (1 Peter ii. 13). Ordinance means law. To submit to a law means to obey it. And then the meaning of this passage is—obey every law of man for the sake of God; or, in other words, we ought to learn to obey because God commands us to do so. And this is the strongest reason we can have. This is the reason why Jesus acted just as He did. God wanted Him to come into our world, and He came. God wanted Him to live at Nazareth, obeying His earthly parents for thirty years, and He did so.

Then, after that, God wanted Him to go about and teach the people, and He did it. God wanted Him to be engaged every day in working miracles and doing good, and He did so. God wanted Him to suffer and to die, and He did suffer and die. God wanted Him to lie in the grave, and He was buried, and did lie in the grave three days. And in doing all this Jesus was thinking about God His Father, and was trying to please Him.

He not only obeyed His *parents*, but obeyed all the Jewish laws. He was baptized, and kept the Sabbath, and did everything that had been written about Him by the prophets; and He did all this for God's sake—because He wanted Him to do it.

And this is the way in which we should learn to obey. God wants us to obey our parents, and the laws of our school, of the family in which we are living, and the laws of our country, and every right law. And we should do this for God's sake—because He wants us to do it. God sends us into this world on purpose that we may learn to obey. When we are obeying our parents and teachers we are pleasing God; when we are disobeying our parents, or breaking the laws that are made for us, we are disobeying God, and doing what He dislikes above all things. God wants us to learn to obey, because He knows that we cannot be happy in any other way.

Is heaven a happy place? Yes. Are the angels who live there happy? Yes. And the reason why they are happy is, because they obey God. We read in the Bible about some of the angels in heaven who refused to obey God, and we know what happened to them. They were driven out of heaven, to be cast into 'everlasting fire, prepared for the devil and his angels.'

Were Adam and Eve happy when they were put into the garden of Eden? Yes. Just so long as they obeyed they were happy. But they disobeyed God. And what happened then? They were driven out from that bright and beautiful place. That was the way in which God punished them for not obeying Him. God does not like to punish people, but when we do not obey Him He is obliged to do it. When we are tempted not to obey, let us think of Jesus. He went down with His parents to Nazareth, and was subject unto them. He went quietly on for thirty years, obeying His parents every day. He did this to set us an example; and now He wants us to follow His example. When we are trying to obey, we are trying to be like Jesus. And so we see that the first reason why we should learn to obey is, *for God's sake*—because He wants us to do it.

The second reason why we should learn to obey is, FOR THE SAKE OF THOSE AROUND US.

A person who has not learned to obey is a dangerous person. He is doing harm all the time to those about him by his example. Let me try to show you how this is.

You know that over in the western part of Europe is a country called Holland. The land in that country lies very low. It is situated near the sea, and a large part of it lies below the level of the sea. You may ask, Why then does not the water of the sea flow over it and cover it? It would do so but for one thing: all along the borders of the sea and the banks of the river the people have built high, strong walls, or embankments. These are made of earth, and are intended to keep back the waters of the sea from overflowing the land. These walls, or dams, as they call them, are very important to the people of Holland. The safety of their lives and property depends on them. The Dutch people, who live in Holland,

THE LESSON OF OBEDIENCE. 27

watch their walls with the greatest care. If they find one of them beginning to give way, and to look as though the water were coming through, they leave off their work,—no matter what they are doing,—and never rest till that part of the wall is made quite strong and safe.

Now, suppose that you and I were living in Holland, near one of those great sea-walls; and suppose we should find out that a person in our neighbourhood was trying to break down that wall and let the sea rush in and drown us, should we not think that *that* was a dangerous person? Why, yes; he would be putting the lives and property of all the people around us in danger. Well, just what those walls or embankments are to Holland, God's laws are to us. They are intended for our protection. When people sin against God, they make Him angry; then He sometimes sends trials or judgments upon them. These trials or judgments are like floods of water that sweep over a place and spread ruin abroad; but God's laws are like walls that keep back the floods or waves of His anger from us. When we obey God, we are trying to build up those walls and strengthen them; but when we disobey God, we are trying to break down those walls. This is the greatest harm we can do. Persons who are doing this are very dangerous persons. But this is just what every boy and girl, and man and woman, is doing who is disobeying God. Such persons are just as dangerous to us as those people would be in Holland who were trying to make holes in the embankments and let the sea come rushing in upon the country.

'Wouldn't you like to be a judge?' said a gentleman one day to a little boy. After thinking about it for a moment, the little fellow said:

'No, sir; I think I would rather teach children about Jesus, who died for them. This would make them love and obey Him; and if they only learned to love and obey Him, they wouldn't need a judge.'

That was a very wise answer.

There is an island on the coast of Virginia, the inhabitants of which get their living by fishing, and catching oysters and clams. For a long time they had neither church nor Sunday-school among them. They were a wicked set of people, and tried to cheat everybody with whom they had any dealings. After awhile a good faithful minister was sent to them. He preached to them about Jesus, and tried to get them to love and obey Him; and no person can do this without being made better. Those who have anything to do with them will find the benefit of it. This was the case with these Virginia fishermen, as was shown by the following incident:

The minister just spoken of was trying to get a new church built, and as the people had not much money, and the minister had once been a carpenter, he took hold and helped to build it himself. One day, as he was busy with his coat off, working away on the church, a stout, hearty-looking sea-captain went by. When he came opposite the church he stopped, and hailed the parson thus:

'Halloa, there, shipmate, are you the minister of this church?'

'I am, sir.'

'Well, then, look here; I've got some money for you.'

'For the church, do you mean, sir?'

'No, sir; not for the church, but for yourself. I like your way of teaching the people here. I've been coming to this island for clams a good many years, and I have always found, when I got home and counted out my cargo, that I was short of what I had paid for by a thousand or fifteen hundred. But since you have been here I've found it very different. If

THE LESSON OF OBEDIENCE. 29

will pay me to have you go on preaching doctrines that will make the people count their clams honestly.'

This is just as it should be. Those fishermen were learning to obey God. And when we properly learn this lesson, it will always make us better than we were before. As the catechism says, it will make us 'true and just in all our dealings.'

There was a good but very strange minister in England once, who used to say that 'he wouldn't give a straw for any man's religion unless his cat and dog were better off for it.' He meant to say that when we learn to obey God, or become truly religious, it will make us better than ever we were before, and kinder to everybody about us. And this is true.

Let us take another illustration to show how important it is to those about us that each of us should try to obey God. Here, for example, is one of those great steamships that are going across the ocean all the time. It is built of iron. This iron is in large sheets. These sheets of iron have holes made all round the different sides of them. Then the edges are put together; iron bolts are put through them, and either hammered out on the other side into rivets, or else fastened by screws. The safety of that great vessel, and of all on board, depends on those rivets and screws. Suppose that while this vessel is out in the middle of the ocean all the rivets should be loosened, and all the screws unfastened. What would happen? She would go to pieces, and sink.

Now, suppose that you and I were crossing the ocean in one of these steamers; and suppose that we found one man among the passengers who spent his time in unfastening the screws and taking out the rivets which kept the vessel together. Would he not be a dangerous passenger? Yes, indeed. We should not think it safe for him to be at liberty. We should tell him that he must either stop that work, or be locked up.

Now, the people who live together in a city like this are like the passengers on board a steamship. God's laws are the things which keep us safe here, just as the rivets and screws are the things that keep the steamship safe. Breaking God's laws is as dangerous a thing to us as loosening the rivets and screws would be to a steamship. It is important for everybody on board that ship that the rivets and screws should be all kept tight, and so it is important to every one in this city and country that God's laws should be obeyed. If I do not try to obey God, I am doing harm to you and to all about you. And it is the same with each of you. If you are not trying to obey God, you are doing harm to me and to all about me. And so you see there is a great deal of force in the reason we are now speaking of. We ought to obey God, in the second place, *for the sake of those around us.*

But, in the third place, we ought to learn to obey FOR OUR OWN SAKES.

God has promised His blessing to those who learn to obey. And there are three things wrapped up in this blessing, which show that the best thing we can do for our own sake is to learn to obey.

There is *happiness* in that blessing which God promises to those who obey.

Let me show you this in the case of a little girl only two years old. Her name was Kitty. She came in from play one warm summer afternoon, and asked her mother for a drink of cool lemonade, that was standing on the table.

'Say please, mamma,' said her mother, as she took up the glass to give it to her.

'Titty tan't say pease,' said the little one. She had said this word a hundred times before, and always

THE LESSON OF OBEDIENCE.

seemed glad to say it; but now, for the first time in her short life, she had made up her mind not to obey. Her mother set the glass down untasted, and Kitty went to the door; but it was very warm, and soon she came running back again, and her thirsty red lips were held up for a drink.

'Say please, Kitty,' said her mother.

'Tan't say pease;' and the baby went away again thirsty.

This was done perhaps half a dozen times during the afternoon, but the little thing would not say please, and so she got no drink.

Supper-time came. Kitty ran up to her high chair, and looked to her mother to lift her into it.

'Say please, Kitty.' Instantly her little face fell. She shook her head, muttered, 'Tan't say pease,' and went away. The rest of the family went on with their supper, but they felt very sadly. They all wanted their little pet to take her usual place with them; but instead of this the rebellious child stood in the corner, pouting and crying, but not willing to obey. After supper her mother took her up to her room, and talked kindly to her, and tried to show her how naughty and wicked it was for her to do so; but still she shook her head, and said, 'Tan't say pease.'

Then Kitty was handed over to her father. He spoke pleasantly to her, and tried everything he could think of to get her to obey; but the end of it was, 'Tan't say pease.' Then a gentle whipping was tried. Such a thing had never been thought of before in connection with Kitty; but it had no effect. She was put to bed without her mother's kiss, a little rebel still.

The morning came, and Kitty remained the same. She stood by her chair at the breakfast table. 'Tan't say pease.' She went without her breakfast. It was getting to be dreadful. Her father and mother were alarmed; but they could not give up. Her brothers and sisters were greatly distressed; but nobody could help her unless she would obey.

Before dinner-time the doctor came in. He heard all about the case, and said: 'Whatever comes of it, you mustn't give up.'

Sometimes he used to take one or other of the children to ride with him. Kitty had never been taken yet. He said to her, 'Kitty, wouldn't you like to take a ride with me?' She jumped at the idea, and began to caper round for joy.

'Well, run ask your mother to please put your hat on,' said the doctor.

In a moment Kitty changed again. With her finger in her mouth, and a downcast look, she said, 'Tan't say pease.' So the doctor had to give up.

And now what was to be done? It was getting towards noon. Kitty's mother was almost heartbroken. The poor child had been twenty-four hours without tasting a mouthful of food. She would not obey, and no one could help her till she did. Everything was standing still in that family. No one could do anything but grieve over Kitty.

Then her mother took her in her arms and carried her up-stairs again. She told her how wicked it was to do so, how displeasing it was to God, and how much sorrow it was causing her parents and brothers and sisters. Then she kneeled down, and prayed God to send His Holy Spirit to change Kitty's heart, and teach her to obey. And just then the poor child gave way. She threw her arms round her mother's neck, and cried, 'Pease—pease—pease—pease!'

How gladly her mother clasped her to her bosom, and covered her with kisses. Then Kitty ran downstairs, and jumped into her father's arms, crying 'Pease, pease, pease!' Oh how happy Kitty was then! And how happy everybody about her was! How they all laughed and cried for joy '

THE LESSON OF OBEDIENCE.

Kitty had *learned to obey*. It brought God's blessing upon her at once. She found that there was happiness in that blessing.

But there is *safety*, as well as happiness, in the blessing which obedience brings.

There was a little girl named Mary. She had a little white dog, called Fido, that she was very fond of. She used to play with him for hours, and took the greatest possible care of him.

One day her mother wished to visit a neighbour, and, fearing that Mary, who was quite a little girl, might go too near the stove, or meet with some accident if left alone in the house, she told her to take Fido and play in the front yard till she came back, but not to go into the house.

She had not been gone long when a large dog came by the gate and turned into the house, through the kitchen door, which stood open. Fido ran in too, to have some fun. But the big dog bit him, and chased him about the kitchen. Poor Fido tried to get away, and yelped for his little mistress to come and help him.

Little Mary was very much distressed. She wanted to save her poor pet Fido, but her mother had told her not to go in, and she had learned to obey.

Pretty soon some children, going home from school, passed by, and told Mary that if she would go with them they would help her to get Fido away from the big dog. But Mary said, 'No, mother told me to stay out here, and I can't go in.'

The children said, when her dog was in such danger, her mother wouldn't care if she did go in 'just for a minute, and come right out again.'

But Mary stood firm: 'Mother said, " *Stay here*," and I can't disobey her.'

And just see what followed. While they were talking about it, some men came hastily into the yard, and asked the children if they had seen a big dog go

c

by. Hearing that he was in the house, they went in and killed him, for the *dog was mad*. He had been running about the country, and had bitten many cattle before he came to Mary's house. It was found that he had killed poor Fido. He would have bitten Mary, and she would have died of that dreadful disease which follows from the bite of a mad dog, if she had not been so careful to obey her mother. Mary had learned to obey. This brought God's blessing on her. She found safety in that blessing.

One day an old man was sitting by the banks of a stream. He looked very sad, and the big tears were rolling down his cheeks. A little boy came running along. He stopped when he saw the old man weeping, and said, 'What makes you cry, sir?'

'Oh, my little man,' said he, 'I have reason enough to cry! This stream reminds me of a great sin that I once committed. When I was a boy I lived in this neighbourhood. I had a dear little sister, named Nellie, whom I loved very much. My sick mother gave her into my care, and told me never to take her near the brink of the river. Mother was sick a long while. Not minding her words, I went one day with Nellie to the river. While I was busy playing she went rambling along the stream, and I had forgotten about her till I heard her wild scream, "Oh, help me! brother, help!" I ran to the place as fast as I could, but it was only to see dear Nellie's little hand, that she had lifted up, sinking out of sight in the river. It was too late.

'How dreadfully I felt! I ran home, screaming, "Nellie is drowned! Nellie is drowned!"

'Mother heard my shrieks. The sudden fright killed her. My mother and sister were put into the same coffin, and buried in the same grave. *My disobedience had killed them both!*'

Poor old man! No wonder that he wept. If

he had only learned to obey, he would have been saved from that great sorrow. God's blessing follows obedience, and there is safety in that blessing.

But there is *success* in the blessing which obedience brings, as well as happiness and safety.

Joseph made up his mind to obey God, and the blessing which followed his obedience brought wonderful success to him. His brothers were unkind to him, and cruelly tore him away from his loving father, and sold him as a slave into Egypt. But he obeyed God among strangers, as he had done at home, and God sent the blessing of success, and he became the governor of all the land of Egypt.

And so it was with David. He made up his mind to obey God when he was a poor shepherd boy, and God's blessing followed him with success, till he became the king of Israel.

We cannot succeed in anything we try to do without God's blessing, and God will not bless those who do not learn to obey.

'*And He went down to Nazareth, and was subject unto them.*'

Jesus spent thirty years in obeying His parents, in order to set us an example of obedience. To learn to obey is the most important lesson for us to learn. There are three great reasons why we ought to learn this lesson.

We ought to learn it, in the first place, *for God's sake;* in the second place, *for the sake of those around us;* and in the third place, *for our own sake.*

God's blessing follows those who learn to obey; and wrapped up in this blessing are happiness, safety, and success.

But remember we cannot obey God of ourselves; and if we want to learn this lesson well, we must ask God to bless us for Jesus' sake, and then we shall be able to follow His example, and obey as He did.

III.

'𝕯𝖊𝖑𝖎𝖛𝖊𝖗 𝖒𝖞 𝖘𝖔𝖚𝖑, 𝕺 𝕷𝖔𝖗𝖉, 𝖋𝖗𝖔𝖒 𝖑𝖞𝖎𝖓𝖌 𝖑𝖎𝖕𝖘.'—Ps. cxx. 2.

IF I take out my watch to find what time it is, it will be of little use for me to look at it unless I am sure that it keeps good time. If it sometimes stands still for an hour or more, and then goes on again; if it sometimes loses two or three hours a day by going too slow, or gains as much more by going too fast, then I cannot depend upon it. A watch that cannot be depended upon is of very little use. It may have a beautiful gold case, it may be sparkling with jewels, but yet it will be of no service to me as a watch unless I can depend on what it tells me about the time. We do not judge of the value of a watch by the kind of case it has, but by finding out whether it keeps good time.

And so one of the things by which we judge of the real value and worth of men or women, of boys or girls, is this—Are they truthful? Do they mean what they say? Are they really what they seem to be? If they speak the truth, and act the truth, then they are like a watch that keeps good time.

But one of the effects of sin on our hearts has been to take away from them the love of the truth, and to incline them to lying. This is one of the symptoms of the dreadful disease of sin. And David in our text shows us how we may get this disease cured; it is by offering the prayer, 'Deliver my soul, O Lord, from lying lips.' Here we have a leaf from the tree of life for the cure of lying. Our subject to-day is— *The lesson of truth; or, the cure of lying.* I wish to speak of three reasons why we should offer this prayer, and try to be delivered from lying lips.

We should do so, in the first place, because of the DISGRACE *which attends lying.*

It is always a good reason to keep from doing anything, if we know that it will really bring shame and disgrace upon us. I do not mean to say that we should be ready to do anything that wicked men want us to do, and that they will try to disgrace us for not doing. If this were so, then we should have to say that Daniel and his three friends were wrong for not being willing to do what the king of Babylon and the wicked men there wanted them to do. And, in the same way, we should have to say that all the martyrs were wrong, who brought persecution and death on themselves for not being willing to do what pleased wicked men. It should make little difference to us what wicked men consider to be disgraceful. But if anything will bring shame and disgrace to us, in the opinion of God and of good men, then we should be very careful not to do *that* thing, whatever it may be. But there is nothing that will do this sooner than lying. If we want to find out whether anything is right or wrong, honourable or dishonourable, the only proper way is to see what God says or thinks about it. His word, or will, or opinion, must be our law in these things. And it is very easy to find out from the Bible what God thinks about lying. It tells us in one place that 'the Lord *hateth* a lying tongue' (Prov. vi. 17). It tells us in another place that 'lying lips are an *abomination* to the Lord' (Prov. xii. 22). And certainly it must be a disgraceful or dishonourable thing to do anything that God hates, or that He speaks of as an abomination to Himself.

But there is another thing that shows us how disgraceful lying is. It is always disgraceful to follow the example of a very wicked person. But we know that Satan is the most wicked person in this world, or in any other. Our Saviour tells us that he is '*the father of lies*' (John viii. 44). When we tell lies, we prove ourselves to be the children of Satan. And there cannot be a greater disgrace in the world than to be closely related to such a person, and to have it proved that he is our father.

But liars are not only the *children* of Satan; they are his *servants* also. When Ananias was trying to deceive the Apostle Peter, he saw through what he was doing, and said unto him, 'Ananias, why hath *Satan filled thine heart* to lie?' (Acts v. 3). Lying is Satan's work. And when we engage in lying, we let our hearts become Satan's workshop. He comes in and carries on his trade there; and we become his apprentices, his workmen, his servants. We lend ourselves to him, and become his tools. We help to do his wicked work in the world. And can there be any greater disgrace than this? No. God considers lying a disgrace; and good men everywhere consider it a disgrace.

In some parts of India they have very strict rules about lying. One of these is rather strange and severe. If any person is proved to be a liar, he receives the penalty of the law, which requires that his mouth be sewed up. The offender has his hands tied behind him. He is led out to a post in a public place, to which he is tied, and one of the officers of the government, appointed for that purpose, sews up his lips with a needle and thread. Then he is allowed to go. And every one who sees his closed lips, and the blood flowing from them, can say to himself, 'There goes a liar!' What a disgrace that sewed-up mouth would be to a man! And when people looked at him, how he would want to turn aside his head, or cover up his face, so that they should not see the mark of shame that was upon him!

Suppose that all the people in this city who are in the habit of lying were to be punished in this way to-night, and were obliged to go out to-morrow, I wonder how many sewed-up mouths we should find in walking through the city? *We* do not always know who are liars, but God knows. And it is remarkable that there are two passages in the Bible which show us that God will deal with liars in a way similar to this. I do not mean that it will be by actually *sewing up* their mouths, but really by closing them, somehow or other. David tells us that 'the mouth of them that speak lies shall be *stopped*' (Ps. lxiii. 11); Solomon tells us that 'a lying tongue is but *for a moment*' (Prov. xii. 19); and in another place David says that 'lying lips shall be put *to silence*' (Ps. xxxi. 18).

We are not told how God will do this; but we may be very sure it will be in some way that will fasten shame and disgrace on those who have not prayed earnestly, as David did, in the language of our text, 'Deliver my soul, O Lord, from lying lips.'

When an artist is painting a picture, and wants to make the back part of it look very dark, it helps him to do this if he paints something very bright in the foreground or front part of the picture. And so it will make the disgrace that attends lying look darker, if we pause here and say something about the honour that follows those who form the habit of always telling the truth.

Little Charlie Foster was playing with his ball in the school-yard one morning before school began. Presently the ball slipped out of his hand sooner than he intended, and went through the window with a crash. The window was broken to fragments, and the ball rolled away into a corner of the school-room.

Charlie was frightened. He was a timid boy, and the teacher, Mr. Trumbull, seemed to him very big, and very stern. But Charlie had been taught to love the truth, and stick to it at all times. He did not think for a moment of trying to hide what was done. So, blushing and trembling, with his heart in his mouth, he started, and ran as fast as he could down the road along which the teacher usually came to school, to tell him all about it. Before long he met the teacher walking rapidly towards the school, and so busy thinking that he did not seem to see the little boy, who was trying to get his attention.

'Mr. Trumbull! Mr. Trumbull! stop a moment, please,' said he.

'Oh, Charlie! Good morning. Why, what's the matter now, my little man?'

'I broke your window, sir, but I didn't mean to. I'm very sorry for it. I did it with my ball, and the ball is in the school-room now.'

'Poor child,' said the teacher, who saw his eyes filled with tears, and a look of great distress in his face. 'So you ran all the way to tell me, did you? You've begun right, Charlie, my boy. Whatever mischief you do, never be afraid or ashamed to tell of it.'

Then, with a light heart, Charlie ran back to the school. None of the boys knew that Charlie had told the teacher about it. They had collected together, and were talking about the broken window, and what the teacher would say, as boys like to do under such circumstances.

After awhile a little fellow named Johnny Thompson found the ball, with C. F.—the initials of Charlie Foster's name—marked on it. He guessed at once who had done the mischief. He was not himself in the habit of confessing when he had done wrong; and, judging of Charlie by himself, he supposed that the teacher knew nothing about who was to blame for the accident, so he held up his hand to show that he wished to speak. 'Well, Johnny, what have you to say?' asked Mr. Trumbull.

'Please, sir, I've found out who broke that 'ere window,' said Johnny, in a way which showed how easy it was for him to break the rules of grammar, if he didn't break the window.

'So have I,' said Mr. Trumbull, 'and a *very honourable* person broke it.'

'A very honourable person!' That made Charlie feel very comfortable. And then the teacher told all the boys how Charlie had come himself to tell about it. He spoke in high terms of him as a boy to be trusted, and of the honour he had gained in this way. Then he showed how different it would have been if he had denied it, and told a lie to hide it. He would have been found out sooner or later, and then he would have been covered with shame and disgrace.

'Deliver my soul, O Lord, from lying lips.' We should use this prayer, in the first place, because of the *disgrace* which attends lying.

We should do so, in the second place, because of the INJURY *that it does.*

The first sin ever committed in our world was a lie. It was in the garden of Eden. Satan was tempting Eve to break God's commandment. He did it by telling her a lie, and getting her to believe it. And now it is impossible for anybody to count up all the injury that has been done by that sin. That one sin was like poisoning a fountain, and then all the water that flows from it is poisoned too. That one sin has caused all the people ever born into our world to have wicked hearts.

That one sin has led to all the sickness and sorrow,

the pain and death, that have been in the world ever since. All the tears that have been shed, all the hearts that have been broken, all the murders that have been committed, all the battles that have been fought, all the violence and misery that have filled the earth for centuries, may be traced up to that one sin, that first lie, just as you trace streams up to the fountain from which they flow.

And when we tell a lie now, we never can tell where the injury that springs from it will stop. It is just like loosening a great rock at the top of a mountain, and letting it go rolling and plunging down the side of the mountain. Nobody can tell how far it will go, nor how much injury it will do before it stops rolling. Telling a lie is like letting a wild beast out of a cage. You never can tell how many people that animal will wound or kill before he is caught again. Telling a lie is like dropping sparks in powder. It is sure to make an explosion, and no one can tell beforehand how much harm *that* will do. Telling a lie is like going out from the plain beaten path into a tangled wood. You never can tell how long it will take you, or how much you must suffer, before you get back again.

A gentleman once asked a deaf and dumb boy, 'What is truth?' He replied by taking a piece of chalk and drawing on the black-board a straight line between two points. Then he asked him, 'What is a lie?' The boy rubbed out the straight line, and drew a zig-zag or crooked line between the same two points. Remember this.

When the Israelites were pursued by the Egyptians, near the Red Sea, you remember God caused the cloud, which had guided them by day, to go and stand between them and their enemies at night. That cloud had two sides. The side towards the Israelites was very bright, while the side towards the Egyptians

THE LEAF FOR CURING LYING. 43

was very dark. And it is just so with most of the illustrations we find on this part of our subject. We can hardly ever see the injury that lying does, without at the same time seeing the good that is done by telling the truth.

Two boys came at an early hour to a country market-town. They spread out their little stands, and sat down to wait for customers. One of them sold melons and fruit, the other dealt in oysters and fish. The market hours passed on, and they were both doing well. The goods on their stands were gradually getting less, and the money in their pockets gradually getting more. The last melon lay on Harry's stand. A gentleman came by, and, placing his hand on it, said, 'What a fine large melon! I think I must buy it. What do you ask for it, my boy?'

'The melon is the last I have, sir, and though it looks very fair, there is an unsound spot on the other side,' said the boy, turning it over.

'So there is,' said the man. 'I think I'll not take it. But,' he added, looking in the boy's face, 'is it very business-like to point out the defects of your goods to customers?'

'Perhaps not, sir, but it's better than being dishonest,' said the boy modestly.

'You are right, my boy. Always remember to speak the truth, and you will find favour with God and man. You have nothing else that I wish this morning, but I shall not forget your little stand in the future.' Then, turning to Ben Wilson's stand, he asked, 'Are those oysters fresh?'

'Yes, sir; fresh this morning,' was the reply. The gentleman bought them and went away.

'Harry, what a fool you were to show the gentleman that spot in the melon! Now you can take it home for your pains, or throw it away. How much wiser I was about those stale oysters! Sold them at the same price as the fresh ones. He would never have looked at the melon till he got home.'

'Ben, I wouldn't *tell* a lie, or *act* one either, for twice the money we've both earned to-day. Besides, I shall be better off in the end, for I have gained a customer, and you have lost one.'

And so it proved; for the next day the gentleman bought a large supply of fruit from Harry, but he did not spend another penny at Ben's stand. So it continued all through the summer. At the close of the season he took Harry into his store, and after awhile gave him a share in the business.

A young man named Evans had a situation in a large warehouse in London. One part of his duty was to arrange the different coloured pieces of goods in the shop window, so as to make them look as attractive as possible. One rainy morning in November he was late in coming to the shop. He went into the window to arrange the goods. Being in a hurry, he slipped. His foot went through the window. It was a large plate-glass window, that cost twenty pounds. He was frightened when he saw what he had done. His first thought was to cover up the broken glass with a piece of goods, say nothing about it, and if charged with doing it, to deny it. But he had promised the friend who recommended him to his place always to tell the truth. He remembered that promise, and resolved to keep it.

When his employer came in, he went at once and told him about the accident, expressed his sorrow for it, and offered to pay for it out of his wages. The gentleman was very angry. He scolded him sharply, and went to his counting-room calling him an awkward, clumsy fellow. 'But,' said he, in talking to the foreman about it, 'Evans is an honest fellow. He's a fellow to be trusted.'

And he *was* trusted. Soon after he found himself

promoted. The promotion went on till he was made foreman of the establishment. Before his employer died, he gave him his daughter—the only child he had —in marriage, and left him heir of all his property. And when he told him he was going to do this, he said to him, ' Evans, this all comes out of that broken window, and your telling the truth about it.'

Here we see how much good was done by telling the truth. But if he had told a lie instead of the truth, the lie would have been found out. He would have lost his character, and lost his situation, and, instead of having that good wife, and that large fortune, would probably have gone to ruin; and all this injury would have come from one lie.

The second reason why we ought to pray to be kept from lying is, because of the *injury* that it does.

The third reason why we ought to pray to be kept from lying is, because of the PUNISHMENT *that follows it.*

God speaks in the Bible very plainly about the punishment that follows lying. He tells us in one place, ' *He that speaketh lies shall perish* ' (Prov. xix. 9). In another place He tells us that ' whatsoever,' or whosoever, ' loveth and maketh a lie shall in no wise enter heaven' (Rev. xxi. 27). And in yet another place He utters these awful words, which are enough to make our flesh creep and our blood run cold, if we commit this sin : '*All liars shall have their part in the lake that burneth with fire and brimstone* ' (Rev. xxi. 8).

But then it is not only after death that punishment follows lying. The Bible shows us how God often punishes people for lying even in this life.

There we see Gehazi telling a lie, and the very same day on which he told it brought the punishment. The dreadful leprosy fastened upon him in a moment, at the word of the prophet Elisha. The prophet said it should ' cleave to him and his children for ever.' If we could find any of the descendants of Gehazi living now, we should find, no doubt, that they had the leprosy in their family still. It is nearly three thousand years since these words were spoken. About a *hundred generations* of Gehazi's children have lived since then, if his family have been continued; and the children of all those generations have been made to feel how dreadful the punishment of lying is. And then we read about Ananias and Sapphira. They agreed together to tell a deliberate, dreadful lie; and they were both struck dead with that lie upon their lips.

And we often see the same punishment following the sin of lying now. In the town of Devizes in England, about a hundred years ago, the following sad event took place:—

Three women, who were neighbours, agreed together to buy a sack of meal. Each of the three was to pay her share of the price. One of the women, in collecting the different sums together, found that there was a certain amount short. She charged Ruth Peirce, one of the three, with keeping back part of the price. Ruth declared that she had paid her full share, and expressed the wish that she might drop down dead if what she said was not true. She wickedly repeated this awful wish, when, to the surprise and horror of the crowd around her,—for this occurred in the marketplace,—she instantly fell down dead, and *the money was found in her hand*. This produced so solemn an impression on the people of that town, that the mayor and corporation had an inscription in stone put in one of the public buildings of the town, telling of the death of this woman, with her name, and the day of the month and the year in which it occurred, as a warning to liars.

Here is another example of the same kind:—

Some time ago, a poor widow woman lived in a small cabin in the county of Galway in Ireland. She had a rent of three pounds a year to pay for her cabin. She was in the habit of paying it every six months; but she often found it very hard to get as much money together. Once, when her rent was coming due, she went to the bank in the neighbouring town to get her thirty shillings changed into a note.

The landlord lived a good way off from her house; but one of her neighbours, a man named Brien, was going to pay his rent to the same person, so she gave him her note and asked him to pay her rent at the same time. He took the note, and said he would gladly do it for her, and save her the trouble of going.

Some time after this, the agent of the landlord called on the poor widow and asked for the rent. She said she had sent it by her neighbour Brien, on the very day that it was due. The agent said it had not been paid. Then he called on Brien; but he denied ever having received the money. The widow was told that she must pay the rent or be turned out of the cottage. It was impossible for her to get so much money again, so she went to law to try and force Brien to give up her money.

The court was opened, and the day of trial came. The judge asked the widow what was the number of the note she gave Brien, and the name of the bank that issued the note. She told him. Then he asked if she had any witness to prove that she gave the note to Brien.

'There was no one present, your honour,' said she, 'but the great God. He was the only one who saw me give it into the man's hands; and I call Him to witness that I am speaking nothing but the honest truth this day.'

Then the judge asked Brien what he had to say. He positively denied it all; but seeing that the poor widow's simple story, and her tears, had made a great impression on the minds of those present, he went on solemnly to say, 'Please, your honour, I never received any money from this woman. I appeal to God, as she has done. May I drop down dead this moment if what I say is not true.'

The words were scarcely out of his mouth when he fell to the floor. This made a great excitement in the court. The man was carried out into the open air, and a physician was sent for. But nothing could be done for him. He never breathed again. With that dreadful lie upon his lips he went into the presence of the God whom he had offended.

When they came to examine the man, they found in one of his pockets the very note which the poor widow had given him.

And so we see there are three good reasons why we should offer the prayer of our text, 'Deliver my soul, O Lord, from lying lips.' We ought to do it, in the first place, because of the *disgrace* which attends lying; in the second place, because of the *injury* which it does; and in the third place, because of the *punishment* that follows it.

Whenever we are tempted to tell a lie, let us remember these three words,—the *disgrace*, the *injury*, the *punishment* of lying,—and then let us pray to God for His help to resist the temptation. Then we shall be delivered from lying lips, and shall learn to love the truth, and keep to it always.

IV.

'So.'—PROV. iii. 10.

THIS is a very short text. It is but one word, and *this* word is one of the smallest in our language. It has only two letters in it. We could not have a shorter word than this. If you try to make it any shorter, it becomes only a letter, not a word. And yet this little word is most important. It is the point on which the whole meaning of two verses turns; and we must look at both these verses if we want to find out the meaning of this little word 'so.' In the verse just before this word, Solomon says: 'Honour the Lord with thy substance, and with the first-fruits of all thine increase.' This means: give something to God out of everything you get. The verse which follows after this word 'so' reads thus: 'So shall thy barns be filled with plenty, and thy presses shall burst out with new wine.' This means: God shall bless thee. And if we put the meaning of these two verses together, we see that what is wrapped up in this little word '*so*' is just this: *Give something to God out of everything you get, and then God will bless you.* And the lesson which this word teaches us is *the lesson of giving*. This is the leaf from the tree of life to cure covetousness. Here we learn the Bible lesson of giving. Our subject now is—*The lesson of giving.*

'*So.*' Give something to God out of everything

you get, and then God will bless you. This is the lesson of giving.

I wish to speak of *three* things that should lead us to learn and practise this lesson of giving.

The first thing that should lead us to learn it is GRATITUDE.

God has given us all that we have; and if we remember this, gratitude for these gifts should make us willing to give to Him whenever we have an opportunity.

One day a gentleman gave a little boy four shillings. 'Now you must keep that,' said the gentleman.

'Oh no!' said the boy. 'I shall halve it first. Maybe I shall keep *my* half.'

'*Your* half!' said the gentleman. 'Why, it's *all* yours.'

'No,' answered the child, with an earnest shake of the head; 'no, it's not all mine; I always go halves with God. Half I shall keep, and half I shall give to Him.'

'God owns the world; He does not need it,' said the gentleman; 'the gold and the silver, and the cattle on a thousand hills, belong to Him.'

The little boy looked puzzled for a moment. He had never thought of this. Presently he said: 'Anyhow, God goes halves with us, and don't you think we ought to give Him back His part?'

That was the right feeling. This little boy felt grateful to God for all the good things He had given him, and it was the gratitude he felt that made him desire to '*go halves with God.*'

But then Jesus gave *Himself* to die for us, and gratitude for this should make it easy for us to learn the lesson of giving.

A gentleman from this country was travelling through France. He attended a Protestant church in the city of Lyons one Easter Sunday. The Lord's Supper was celebrated. After it was over, a collection was taken up to help them to build a new church. Instead of having the collection boxes handed round as we do, a table was placed in front of the chancel, and one by one the members of the congregation came up and laid upon it whatever they had to give. Among the rest, a soldier came up. The tear of gratitude was trickling down his face as he laid on the table all his earnings for the last three months. The minister knew the man, and knew his circumstances, and fearing that he was giving more than he could afford, asked him if he could spare as much as that.

'Spare it!' said the soldier, with deep feeling. ' My blessed Saviour spared not *Himself*, but freely gave His life for my redemption, and surely I can spare one quarter of my year's earnings for the promotion of His glory here on earth.'

This is the true feeling to have; and if we all felt as this pious soldier did, we should find it very easy to learn, and very pleasant to practise, the lesson of giving.

This feeling in our hearts will make the *least* offering we have to present acceptable to God, while the *largest* that any one can give will be of no value to Him without this feeling.

They were taking up a collection for foreign missions one day at a village church in England. The richest man in the village walked up and laid down a five-pound note on the plate. The people admired the gift, and praised the giver; but God was not pleased with it.

Directly after him came up a poor little pale-faced girl, meanly clad, and with thin, pinched, half-starved-looking features, which told of her great poverty. Yet her countenance was full of sweetness, and a tear was trembling in her eye as she laid beside the rich man's note a single penny. The crowd pushed her rudely by. No one noticed or cared for her gift. But to Jesus, and the angels who were looking on, it was far more precious than the large gift of the rich man.

And that which made the difference between these two offerings was the feeling which prompted them. Before the rich man left home that morning he said to himself: 'What shall I give to the collection for foreign missions to-day? I must give a five-pound note. This is what will be expected of me, and I wish to give a larger offering than any one else.'

On that same morning the little girl had been reading her Bible, as she was in the habit of doing. She had learned about the love of Jesus, and she oved Him in return. She thought within herself: 'If Jesus did so much for me, what can I do to show my love for Him? There is to be a collection for foreign missions to-day. A penny is *all* I have; but I will give my penny for Jesus' sake. He will accept it from me, because I love Him so much.' Then she took her penny and laid it on the chair before which she was kneeling, and prayed for a blessing on it, thus: 'O my Saviour, here is a penny which I wish to give to Thee. It is all I have. Take it, Lord, although I am not worthy to give it, and bless it, so that it may do good to the heathen. For Thy name's sake, amen.'

Then, rising from her knees, she took it to the church and laid it on the plate.

The love or gratitude which led her to give that penny made it very precious in God's sight.

And we feel just the same way towards those who offer us presents. If we know that a person really loves us, we prize the least thing that person gives us; but if a person that we know does not love us offers us a present, we care very little about it, even though it may be quite valuable.

A poor labouring man had raised a turnip in his garden which was so remarkably large that every one wondered at its great size.

'I will present it to the squire of our village,' said he, 'because he has been so kind to me, and because he is always pleased to see us cultivating our fields and gardens.'

He took the turnip up to the castle. The squire praised the man for his industry and care, and gave him three sovereigns. A selfish, money-loving peasant of the same village heard of this, and said, 'Ah, I will make the squire a present of my finest calf. If he gives my neighbour three golden pieces for a turnip, how much will he give me for my fine calf?' He led the calf by a rope to the castle, and asked the squire to accept it as a present. The squire saw at a glance the selfishness of the man, and declined to receive the calf. But the peasant urged him not to refuse his present.

At length the squire wisely said, 'As you are so pressing, I will accept the present; and since you are so generous towards me, I must not be stingy. I will therefore make you a present in return, which cost me three times as much as your calf is worth.'

Then he gave the astonished man the turnip which the peasant had brought him. And the selfish fellow went back to his home mortified and ashamed to think that he had lost his fine calf, and got nothing in return for it but a huge turnip, not worth sixpence.

The turnip was offered to the squire from love and gratitude. *That* made it a golden gift in his eyes. The calf was offered from selfishness, and that made it good for nothing to him. And just so God judges of our offerings.

A poor blind girl in England brought to a clergyman thirty shillings for the missionary cause. He declined to take them, saying, 'You are a poor blind girl, and can't afford to give so much.'

'I am blind indeed, but that's the very reason why I can afford to give these thirty shillings better than you suppose.'

'How so?' asked the minister.

'I am, sir, by trade a basket-maker, and can work as well in the dark as in the light. Now, I am sure that, during last winter, it must have cost those girls who have eyes more than thirty shillings for candles to work by. All this I saved. I love my precious Saviour, and want to do something to show my love for Him. Please take my offering.'

Of course the minister took her gift. And Jesus accepted it. It was the offering of grateful love. That is sure to make everything acceptable to Him. 'So.' This means that we must give something to God out of everything we get, and then God will bless us. The first thing that should lead us to learn and practise this lesson of giving is *gratitude.*

'So.' *The second thing that should lead us to learn and practise this lesson of giving is* DUTY.

This text is God's *command* to us about giving. And when God commands us to do anything, then it becomes our duty to do it. But this is not the only command that God has given on the subject. There are a great many more in the Bible. We find them scattered all over it. Our text is an Old Testament command about giving. And there are other commands of the same kind in the Old Testament, such as these: 'Every man shall give as he is able, according to the blessing which the Lord hath given thee' (Deut. xvi. 17); 'The poor shall never cease out of the land: therefore *I command* thee, saying, Thou shalt open thine hand to the poor and the needy in thy land'

(Deut. xv. 11); 'Cast thy bread upon the waters, for thou shalt find it after many days' (Eccles. xi. 1); 'Deal thy bread to the hungry, and bring the poor that are cast out to thine house' (Isa. lvii. 7).

And then in the New Testament we have many commands of the same kind. Here are some of our Saviour's commands about giving: 'Give to him that asketh' (Matt. v. 42); 'Freely ye have received, freely give' (Matt. x. 8); 'Give alms of such things as ye have' (Luke xi. 41); 'He that hath two coats, let him impart to him that hath none; and he that hath meat, let him do likewise' (Luke iii. 11); 'Upon the first day of the week let every one of you lay by him in store, as God hath prospered him' (1 Cor. xvi. 2); 'Charge them that are rich in this world, that they be ready to give and glad to distribute' (1 Tim. vi. 17, 18); 'To do good and to distribute forget not: for with such sacrifices God is well pleased' (Heb. xiii. 16).

And when we consider all these commands about giving, we have the best reason for trying to learn this lesson of giving. It is our *duty* to do so.

Now let us look at some examples to show us how people give who understand God's command about giving, and are trying to do their duty in this respect.

Here is a good story about the first ripe strawberries.

A little girl once had a bed of strawberries. She was very anxious that they should ripen and be fit to eat. At last the time came.

'Now for a feast!' said her brother to her one morning, as he picked some beautiful berries for her to eat.

'I can't eat these,' she said, 'for they are the first ripe fruit.'

'Well,' said her brother, 'all the more reason for our making a feast, for they are so much the greater treat.'

'Yes, but they are the *first ripe fruit.*'

'Well, what of that?'

'Why, you know the Bible says we must "honour the Lord with all our first-fruits." And dear father says that he always gives God the first out of all the money he gets, and that then he always feels happier in spending the rest; and so I wish to give God the first of my strawberries too.'

'Ah, but,' said her brother, 'how can you give strawberries to God? And even if you could, He wouldn't care for them.'

'Oh, but I've found out a way! You remember how Jesus said, "*Inasmuch as ye have done it unto one of the least of these my brethren, ye have done it unto me.*" So I mean to take them to Mrs. Perkin's dying child. She never gets strawberries, they're so poor.'

Then away ran the children to give the strawberries to the dying child; and when they saw her put out her thin, white arms, and take the ripe, round, juicy fruit in her little shrivelled fingers, and when they saw her eyes glisten, and her little faded lips smile, they felt as if they had a far richer treat than if they had kept the ripe fruit for themselves; and they were sure that God had accepted their offering.

I have one more story about the duty of giving. This may be called giving like a child.

'Not long since a poor widow came to my study,' said a minister of the gospel. 'She is over sixty years of age. Her home is a little room, about ten feet by twelve. She supports herself by her needle. Imagine my surprise when she put twelve shillings in my hands, and said, "There is my contribution to the church fund."

' "But you are not able to give so much," I said.

' "Oh yes!" she exclaimed; "I have learned to give now."

' " How is that ? " I asked.

' " Do you remember," she answered, " that sermon three months ago, when you told us you did not believe that any of your people were so poor, that, if they loved Christ, they could not find some way of showing that love by their gifts ? "

' " Yes, I remember it."

' " Well, I went home and cried all night over that sermon. I said to myself, ' My minister don't know how poor I am, or he never would have said that.' But from crying at last I got to praying ; and when I had told Jesus all about it, I seemed to get an answer in my heart that dried up all my tears."

' " What was the answer ? " I asked, deeply moved by her simple story.

' " Only this : ' If you can't give as other people do, give like a child ; ' and I have been doing it ever since. When I have a penny change from my sugar or loaf of bread, I lay it aside for Jesus, and so I have gathered this money all in pennies."

' " But haven't you suffered from laying aside so much ? "

' " Oh no ! " she said eagerly, and with a pleasant smile. " Since I began to give to the Lord I have always had money in the house for myself, and it is wonderful how the work comes pouring in."

' " But didn't you always have money in the house ? " I asked.

' " Oh no ! Often when my rent came due I had to go and borrow the money, not knowing how I should ever find means of paying it back ; but I don't have to do that any more now."

' Of course I could not refuse such money. Three months later she came again with sixteen shillings, saved in the same way. Then came the special effort of our church in connection with the Memorial Fund, and in about five months she brought three pounds, all saved in the little mite box I had given her; and she was happier that year than I had ever known before. This woman had learned the lesson of giving taught us in the text. She felt the *duty* of giving. The second thing that should lead us to learn this lesson is *duty.*'

'So.' *The third thing that should lead us to learn the lesson of giving is* PROFIT.

Solomon tells us in our text that God's blessing rests on those who learn and practise the Bible rule of giving, which is here taught; and we know that it is God's blessing which makes people truly rich. Anything that fills a man's barns with plenty, and makes his presses burst out with new wine, will be a profit to him, and help to make him rich. The Bible teaches that God's way of making us rich is to have us learn to give. This is the meaning of such passages as these: '*There is that scattereth, and yet increaseth*' (Prov. xi. 24); '*The liberal soul shall be made fat*' (Prov. xi. 25); '*Give, and it shall be given unto you; good measure, pressed down, and shaken together, and running over, shall men give into your bosom*' (Luke vi. 38). These passages all teach us the same lesson that we are taught by this little word '*so.*' They show us that *doing good* is the best way of *getting good;* and that the surest way of getting truly rich is to learn to give as God teaches us to do in the Bible. If we give something to God out of everything we get, then God will bless us, and God's blessing will make us rich. This is the meaning of this little word '*so*' in the verse in which it is found; and this is what the Bible teaches throughout; and there are plenty of illustrations to show that this is true. Let us look at some of these illustrations.

There is a good story told of a certain Christian bishop, who was noted for liberality. One day he was on a journey with his servant. Some poor people applied to them for help. The bishop told his man to give them all the money they had in their purse, which was three silver crowns; but the servant thought he knew better than his master, so he only gave them two, and kept the other crown, as he told his master, to pay for their lodging at night.

Soon after this a rich nobleman met the bishop, and knowing what a good and charitable man he was, he ordered his steward to give two hundred crowns to the bishop's servant for his master's use. As soon as he received the money he ran with joy to tell his master about it.

'Ah,' said the bishop, 'you see how wrong you were in not giving the three crowns to those poor people, as I told you. If you had done this, we should have received three hundred crowns from our friend, instead of two hundred.'

And no doubt he was right in saying this; for it was God that put it into the heart of the nobleman to give this money to the bishop, and he could as readily have put it into his heart to give three hundred as two.

This was in keeping with the word '*so*' in our text, and it shows us what profit there is in giving.

Some years ago a poor boy was in search of a situation. He made many inquiries without finding a place. At last, when he was just on the point of returning home disappointed, a gentleman, who was pleased with his appearance, gave him work. After trying him for some time, he took him as an apprentice. The boy behaved so well during his apprenticeship, that when the time was out his employer lent him money enough to set up business for himself. He felt very thankful for this; and as he was a Christian young man, he made a solemn promise that he would give one-tenth of all the money earned to God. The first year he earned one hundred pounds, and he gave away ten. He kept on faithfully doing this, till his gifts in the course of the year amounted to over five hundred pounds.

Then he began to think that this was a great deal of money to give away, and there was no need of being so particular about it. He ceased giving a tenth of all he made, and that year he lost a ship at sea. This led him to repent, and go back to his former resolution to give God one-tenth of all he earned. *Then* he prospered again, and went on successfully in all he did, till he had made enough money to give up business. For some time after this he still continued to give away the tenth of all his income; but after awhile he became acquainted with some men who did not believe the Bible. They persuaded him that it was foolish to give away so much of his money. He stopped giving as he had promised to do. The end of the matter was that he lost all his property, and died at last a poor man.

Here we see how true the word '*so*' is in our text; how certain it is that God will bless us if we learn to give properly, and how he will withhold that blessing when we refuse to give. This proves that there is profit in giving.

Some years ago there was a widow woman in England, with two children. She made a living for herself and children by taking charge of a lighthouse on the coast.

She was a good Christian woman, but very poor. The church that she attended was engaged in missionary work, and she wanted to do something to help them in this work; but she had very little money to give, and she knew not what to do. Almost every day people came to visit the lighthouse, and when she had shown them through it they generally gave her something for her trouble. In this way she got a good deal of money in the course of the year. After thinking it over a good while, she made up her mind that she would set apart Monday of every week as her missionary day, and all the money received on that day from visitors to the lighthouse she would consider as belonging to God, and would give it to the church for their missionary work. This was her plan, and she resolved to begin on the next Monday.

Well, Monday came. During the morning there were no visitors at the lighthouse. About the middle of the afternoon a good-looking gentleman came to see the lighthouse. She took him all over it, and showed him everything he wanted to see. When he was going away he thanked her for her kindness, and slipped something into her hand. After he was gone she looked at it, supposing it was a shilling, when to her surprise she found it was a gold sovereign. This was more than she had ever received from a visitor before. It was a large sum of money for her to have. It would get some things that she needed very much for the children. She began to question whether she ought to give away so much money. She consulted some of her neighbours about it. They advised her to give one or two shillings to the church, and keep the rest for herself. But not feeling satisfied to do this, after praying over it she resolved to give all to God, according to her promise, and she did so.

The next day a lady with her little daughter came in a handsome carriage to visit the lighthouse. They spoke very kindly to the poor widow, and when they were going away the lady handed her daughter something to give to the keeper of the lighthouse, and when they were gone she found it was a twenty-pound note. That lady was the Duchess of Kent, and her daughter was Victoria, who is now the loved and honoured Queen of England.

That poor widow found that there was profit in giving. She learned that there was a great deal of meaning in this little word '*so*.' She 'honoured the Lord' by giving to Him as she had promised to do, and God blessed her for doing it.

And now we see this little word '*so*,' which we have taken for our text to-day, teaches us the lesson of giving. And the Bible lesson of giving is this: that we must give something to God out of all that we get, and then God will bless us. We have spoken of three things that should lead us to learn this lesson: these are—*gratitude, duty,* and *profit.*

In asking us to give, God is only asking us to follow His example. God is the greatest giver. He is giving all the time. He gives us life and breath, and all things. He never stops giving for a single moment. He gave His Son for us; and He has surrounded us by striking examples of giving. We have examples of giving both *in* the Bible and *out* of the Bible. Look at these examples all around us:

> 'The sun gives ever, so the earth,
> What it can give, so much 'tis worth;
> The ocean gives in many ways,—
> Gives baths, gives fishes, rivers, bays;
> So, too, the air,—it gives us breath,—
> When it stops giving, in comes death.
>   Give, give, be always giving;
>   Who gives not, is not living.
>   The more we give,
>   The more we live.'

'Honour the Lord with thy substance, and with the first-fruits of all thine increase: *so* shall thy barns be filled with plenty, and thy presses shall burst out with new wine.' Remember this little word '*so*,' and the lesson of giving which it teaches. *We must give something to God from all we get, and then He will bless us.*

V.

'*Let patience have her perfect work.*'—Jas. i. 4.

SUPPOSE we have a visit to a photographer's, to see how the pictures are taken there. We find a person sitting in a chair. He is going to have his likeness taken. The photographer arranges his dress, and sees that he is in a proper position. Then he looks into the camera. If he finds everything right, then he puts in the prepared plate, and says, 'All ready?' He raises the curtain from the end of the tube to let the light in, and in a few seconds the likeness is taken. The *sun* has painted that picture; but it has been done in a very different way from that in which men make pictures. The sun paints at the same time nose and mouth, eyes, ears, hair, hands, and dress. But when men paint a picture they are very slow about it. It takes them a long time to do it, and they can only attend to one thing at a time. When they are painting the eye, or the nose, or the mouth, they are not able to do anything else at the same time. They must finish one thing before they can take up another. And if a man wants to be a good painter, he will have to work a long time, and try hard. He should study the best pictures he can find, and try to copy them, not only once, but many times, before he succeeds in getting a good copy.

And this is just what we have to do in trying to become Christians. We are like painters who go to a gallery filled with beautiful pictures, and try to imitate them. The Bible is our picture gallery. It is full of models, or examples of the best kind of characters. We must take these one by one, study them carefully, and try to make ourselves like them. The study now before us is patience. Our subject to-day is—*The lesson of patience.*

'Let patience have her perfect work.' This is a leaf from the tree of life for the cure of impatience. I wish to speak of three reasons why we should learn this lesson of patience.

We ought to learn this lesson, in the first place, because of THE COMFORT IT GIVES.

Patience means not getting put out when things do not turn out just as we wish. Look at Job. He loses his property and children all in one day. This was very hard; yet, instead of fretting or worrying, he bowed himself before God, and meekly said, 'The Lord gave, and the Lord hath taken away, blessed be the name of the Lord.' Here we see the patience of Job.

Look at Abraham. He has just received that strange command to 'take his only son Isaac, whom he loves, and offer him up for a burnt-offering.' How hard this was! But he never stops to complain or argue against it. Instead of this, he goes at once to do it. Here we see the patience of Abraham.

And then look at Jacob. He has just left his father's house in Hebron. There he had been accustomed to good company, and to all the comforts of home. At the close of the first day's journey he finds himself alone, in a strange land. Night overtakes him in the fields of Bethel; he finds no bed but the cold ground, no covering but the far-off sky, no pillow but a stone. Yet without a murmur he quietly lies down to sleep. Here we see the patience of Jacob.

THE LESSON OF PATIENCE.

An old proverb says, 'Patience is the remedy for all troubles.' The best remedy for hard times is patience. In the examination of a school in Scotland, a class was asked this question, What is patience? A little girl in the class answered, 'It is *wait a wee and dinna weary.*' This means to wait and not get tired. Patience is like oil poured on the stormy waters, making them smooth. Patience stifles anger, and sweetens the temper, and subdues pride. Patience bridles the tongue, so that it shall not speak in anger, and holds back the hand from striking in wrath. Patience makes us humble in prosperity, and cheerful in adversity. Patience comforts the poor, and restrains the rich. Patience teaches us to forgive those who have injured us, and to be the first to ask forgiveness of those we have injured. Patience is one of the brightest jewels that can adorn the Christian. She is like a beautiful angel, whose presence brings calm, comfort, and peace wherever she goes.

Now let us look at one or two instances of persons who have learnt this lesson of patience well, and we shall see how much comfort it gave them.

There was a learned judge who used every day to pass by an apple-stand, kept by a good old Christian woman, whose name was Molly. The judge often bought apples from the old woman, and he liked to talk with her. 'Well, Molly,' said the judge, as he stopped one day, 'don't you get tired sitting here these cold dismal days?'

'It's only a little while,' says Molly.

'And the hot dusty days?' said he.

'It's only a little while,' was the answer.

'And the rainy, drizzly days?' said the judge.

'It's only a little while,' was Molly's reply.

'And your sick rheumatic days?' said the judge.

'It's only a little while, sir,' was all that Molly would say.

'Well, Molly, when the "little while" is over, what then?'

'Oh, then, sir,' said Molly with great warmth; 'then I shall enter into the rest that remaineth for the people of God, and the troublesomeness of the way will be forgotten then! It's only a little while, sir.'

'All's well that ends well, I dare say,' said the judge; 'but what makes you so sure about it, Molly?'

'How can I help being sure, sir,' said she, 'since Christ is the Way and I am in Him? He is mine, and I am His. Now I can only feel along the way. I shall see Him as He is in a little while, sir.'

'Ah, Molly, you've learned more than the law ever taught me,' said the judge.

'Yes, sir, because I went *to the gospel*.'

'Well, Molly, I must look into these things,' said the judge, buying an apple and walking off.

'There's only a *little while*, sir, for that; and we are not quite sure of having even a little while,' said she.

This poor woman had learned the lesson of patience, and she had learned it well. Patience was having its perfect work in her. And it made her very comfortable. As she sat at the corner of the street, exposed to the heat of summer and the cold of winter; or as she went back at night to the lonely, cheerless garret which she called her home, she was happier far than the judge, with all his learning and all his money.

During the late war a chaplain in one of the regiments was suddenly stricken down with fever. He was taken to one of the division hospitals. It was his first experience of sickness away from home. How he longed to be at home! Many a time he had taken his seat by the cot of a sick soldier longing for home, and had said, 'Only trust in Jesus, and He will take care of you here, as well as if you were at home.' But now he found how much easier it was to preach than to practise.

Night found him sleepless, alone, and sad. He could not feel patient, or satisfied with God's will. He mourned, like the Jews of old who 'murmured in their tents.' While he lay thus, restless on his cot, as the morning dawned the fold of his tent parted, and a black face peeped through. It was 'Old Nanny,' a coloured woman, who had taken his washing the day before. Looking at the chaplain, she said:

'Massa, does ye see de bright side dis mornin'?'

'No, Nanny,' said he; 'I'm sorry to say I don't see anything bright about it.'

'Well, massa, I allers see de bright side.'

'You do?' said he. 'Maybe you haven't had much trouble?'

'Mebby not,' said Nanny. Then she went on to tell him, in her simple, touching way, of her former life in Virginia, the selling of her children one by one, and the auction sale of her husband and of herself. She was alone now in the world, and had not heard of her family for years.

'Mebby I ain't seen no trouble, massa?'

'But, Nanny,' said the sick man, 'have you seen the bright side *all the time?*'

'Allers, massa, allers.'

'Well, how did you do it?'

'Dis is de way, massa: when I see de great brack cloud comin' over,' and she waved her dark hand inside the tent, as though a cloud was settling down there, 'an' 'pears like it's comin' crushin' down on me, den I just whips aroun' on de oder side, an' I find de Lord Jesus dar; an' den it's all bright an' cl'ar. De bright side is allers whar Jesus is, massa.'

'Well, Nanny,' said he, 'if *you* can do that, I think *I* ought to.'

"'Pears like ye ought to, massa, an' you's a preacher of de word of Jesus.'

The good old darkie went away. The chaplain turned in his cot, and said in his heart, '" The Lord is my shepherd, I shall not want." Come life, come death, come burial on the Yazoo Bluff or in the quiet churchyard at home, " Thy will be done."' He saw the bright side then. Thus learning the lesson of patient submission, he was comforted.

In this sweet spirit of confidence in God's care, willing to let God do with him what He pleased, he slept. When he awoke he was in a profuse perspiration. The fever was broken. He soon got well. Old Nanny's example had taught him the lesson of faith and patience.

We ought to learn the lesson of patience, in the first place, because of the *comfort* it gives.

In the second place, we ought to learn this lesson because of THE GOOD IT DOES.

When a ship is going to sea, it is necessary for her to be properly ballasted. If she has no ballast she will be unsteady; and when the sea is rough, and the wind blows strong, then the vessel, with all on board, will be exposed to danger and destruction. But patience is to the soul like ballast to the ship. The ballast steadies the vessel, and enables her to meet the storms and billows in her way with safety. This shows us what good patience can do.

You remember when the Israelites started on their journey through the wilderness, they came to a well at a place called Marah, which means bitter. Wearied by travel in that hot and sandy desert, their thirst was great, and they longed for water. But, alas! that water was so bitter that they could not drink it. Then God showed Moses a tree which he was to cast into the well, and which made the water sweet, and they found it good.

That tree was just like patience, which has the power to change those troubles which make bitter the waters of life, and sweeten them.

Some one has tried to show the good that is done by patience in this way. He says: There was a meeting called once of all the chief men in a certain country, to try and find out what was the best way of making things better in the world. It was a great meeting. Kings and princes, lawyers and doctors, and philosophers and soldiers, and men of all kinds were there. They had a great time consulting together. In vain they talked, and argued, and planned. No two of them could agree as to the best way of getting rid of the troubles in the world.

One man said the best way was to laugh at everything that happened. Another believed it would be better to cry over everything; while a third was of opinion that it was best neither to laugh nor cry, nor care much about them. The fourth had a different plan from the other three; and the fifth another, which he thought the best of all. The longer they talked, the greater the excitement and confusion.

At last a venerable, grey-haired man, well known for his piety, arose. He said he had a remedy of wonderful power, which he wished them all to use. They tried his remedy, and soon became calm and still. 'My friends,' said he, 'this remedy is called patience. It has a wonderful power over those who use it. You see what an effect it has had upon us. Now, take my advice: use this remedy every day. It will not save you from the troubles that are in the world; but it will help you to meet them in such a way that they will do you good. This is the best way of trying to make things better in the world.' This story, though only a fable, shows the good that patience does.

We have just had an illustration from an assembly

of great men about the use of patience, now let us take another from a barn-yard.

'I learned a good lesson once,' said a Christian lady, 'in a barn-yard. It was a cold frosty morning. I was looking out of a window into the barn-yard, where a great many cows, oxen, and horses were waiting to be watered. For a while they all stood very quiet and still. Presently one of the cows, in attempting to turn round, happened to hit her next neighbour. In a moment this cow kicked *her* neighbour. She passed on the kick to the next. And directly the whole herd were kicking and biting each other with great fury. I laughed to myself, and said, "See what comes of kicking when you are hit!"'

And just so we often see one cross word set a whole family of children to quarrelling. Now, if we feel impatient or cross when we are spoken to, let us remember how the fight began in the barn-yard. A little patience will save us from a great deal of trouble. Here we see the use of patience.

When a *man* breaks his leg, the doctor comes and attends to it. He sets the broken parts of the bone together, and puts splinters on it, and wraps bandages tightly round it. Then the man has to lie by for a number of weeks, keeping quiet and still all the time. In this way the broken bone knits together, and the leg gets well, and is as strong as ever it was. But suppose it is a *horse* that breaks his leg instead of a man. Does the doctor come with his splinters and bandages to bind up the horse's leg? No. It is all over with the horse when *he* breaks his leg. No matter how valuable he is, there is nothing to be done but to shoot him. But what makes the difference between the horse and the man? If the horse's leg could be bandaged and kept still, don't you think it would get well as soon as the man's? Certainly it would. The only difficulty is that the horse cannot

THE LESSON OF PATIENCE. 71

be made to understand the need of patience. He won't keep still. He will keep kicking with his poor broken leg; and this plays the mischief with it, and prevents it from getting well. And so you see that a broken leg, which costs a man only a few weeks' confinement, will cost a horse his life. And the thing which makes the difference is—patience. Then how much good patience does!

'Oh, George Hays, just look here!' said little Anna Almer. 'The old grey cat has jumped through this window, and broken Cousin Alice's beautiful rose geranium. Oh, isn't it too bad? How angry Alice will be!'

'My sister don't get angry at such things, Anna,' said George. 'I never saw her angry but once in my life, and that was when some boys worried a poor little kitten almost to death.'

'But this is so provoking, Georgy. Anybody would be angry.'

'It is really too bad, but you'll see if Alice doesn't try and make the best of it.'

'Perhaps she may,' said Anna; 'but I don't see how it can be done.'

Pretty soon Alice came into the room. Her sunny face was beaming with the cheerful spirit that reigned within. She was humming a tune, but she stopped suddenly before her beautiful yet broken geranium. 'Ah, who has done this?' she cried.

'That ugly old cat broke it, Cousin Alice,' said Anna; 'I saw her myself.'

'Poor puss, she didn't know what mischief she was doing. It was the very pet of all my flowers. But come, little cousin, don't look so long-faced about it; we must try and make the best of it.'

'I don't see that there is any best about this,' said Anna.

'Oh yes, there is! It is not nearly as bad as it

might be. The large stalk is not injured, and it will soon put forth new shoots. This large broken branch will be lovely to make bouquets of. Let us arrange a posy for mother's room. We will put this cluster of scarlet blossoms in a wine-glass, and you may run into the garden and gather a few snowdrops to put with them. There now, was there ever anything prettier? Now we will set the wine-glass in this little saucer, and arrange some geranium leaves around the edge, with more snowdrops mingled among them. You know, dear, how fond mother is of flowers, and how she always thanks God for them. Now, my little cousin, don't you think there is a bright side to this accident? I am not sure but that pussy did us a favour by giving pleasure in an unexpected way.'

'I think you have found the bright side, Alice, but I never could have done it. I almost wanted the old cat killed.'

'There is a bright side to everything, my dear Anna,' said Alice, 'if we only have patience to seek for it, and ask God to help us. Always look for the bright side. It will save you much sorrow through life, and will be like the famous stone which so many have sought for, that was to turn everything into gold.'

Surely it is wise to learn the lesson of patience, as it will help us to see the bright side in everything that happens.

Two gardeners had their crops of peas killed by the frost. One of them was very impatient under the loss, and fretted about it. The other patiently went to work to plant a new crop. After awhile the impatient man came to visit his neighbour. To his surprise, he found another crop of peas growing finely. He asked how this could be.

'This crop I sowed while you were fretting,' said his neighbour.

'But don't you ever fret?' he asked.

'Yes, I do; but I put it off till I have repaired the mischief that has been done.'

'Why, then you have no need to fret at all.'

'True,' said his friend; 'and that's the reason why I put it off.'

We ought to learn the lesson of patience, in the second place, because of the *good* it does.

But there is a third reason why we should try to learn this lesson, and that is because of THE HELP WE HAVE *in doing so.*

We have great help given, in seeking to learn this lesson, from the examples of those who have learned and practised it before us. Suppose we are trying to climb up a steep mountain. We find it very hard work. If we see no footprints of others, we may say, 'No one has ever been along this path before. Perhaps it is impossible to reach the top of the mountain. What is the use of trying?' We feel discouraged, and cease striving. But if the path is well worn, and there are footprints, we know that many people have gone up the mountain; then we may feel encouraged to keep on climbing to the very top.

And so, when we have examples of those who have learned the lesson of patience, and in whom 'patience has had its perfect work,' then we may feel encouraged to try and learn this lesson for ourselves. The missionaries of the gospel, who have gone into heathen lands to teach the people and preach about Jesus, have sometimes met with so many trials and difficulties, and have had to work so long before they could see any result from their labour, that the example of their patience should be as useful as it is remarkable. In every part of the missionary field we have good examples of patience.

Dr. Judson laboured in Burmah for *seven years* before he could see any good resulting from his work. In New Zealand the missionaries laboured for *nine* years before a single heathen was baptized. In Eastern Africa, it was *ten* years; in Western Africa, *fourteen* years; with the Moravians in Greenland, *fifteen* years; and in the island of Tahiti, *sixteen* years, before the missionaries saw the least sign of good for their encouragement. These are wonderful examples. And when we feel impatient and discouraged because we do not succeed at once in what we try to do, let us think of these missionaries labouring patiently on through all those dark and toilsome years, and let their example encourage us in learning the lesson of patience.

Mr. Poole was the writer of a large work on the Bible. It is called *Poole's Synopsis*, and contains the opinions of a great many different writers on the most important passages of the Bible. This work was published in nine large volumes. It took Mr. Poole sixteen years to write these books. And while he was engaged in writing them he always rose at five o'clock in the morning, and then wrote till the close of day, with a short interval for meals. Then he would leave his study, talk with his family, and see his friends. After labouring in this way for sixteen years, he finished this great work. Then he visited his friends to enjoy a little rest and change. While absent, his wife—who was an ill-tempered woman, and was angry with him for a trifling matter—gathered up his papers, and threw them all into the fire. On his return he learned, to his great grief, that the result of his long and patient labour had been burned, and had gone up the chimney in smoke. When he discovered his great loss, he quietly said, 'My dear, you have done very wrong.' The next morning he patiently went to work, and kept on till he had written over again all that his wife had burned. An example like this ought to be a great help in learning the lesson of patience.

Here is an interesting example of patience exercised

towards an idiot boy, and of the blessed results that followed.

This boy was taken to a lunatic asylum to see if anything could be done for his improvement. The asylum was under the care of Christian people, who were patient and persevering in their efforts to benefit the inmates. Three pictures were taken of this boy. The first represented his condition when placed in the institution. Then he appeared to be a hopeless idiot. He was always on the floor, rolling over and over, with his mouth wide open and his tongue lolling out. There was not a ray of intelligence about him, and he seemed more like a beast, without a soul, than a human being. In this state he continued for six months after entering the asylum. So feeble-minded did he appear, that the teachers saw nothing in him to work upon.

One day the wife of the physician having charge of the asylum accidentally dropped her thimble near Jimmey, as the boy was called. He stared at it for a moment, and then grunted out 'Ugh!' This was the first sound he had ever uttered. The delighted wife rushed to her husband to tell him the great fact that Jimmey had said 'Ugh!'

For three long months after this the thimble was dropped every day, in the same place, before the poor boy, and it was always noticed by him with the same 'Ugh!' But nothing else followed for three months. Then one day when the thimble was dropped Jimmey put out his hand and touched it. This was a great step. At the end of the year the second picture of Jimmey was taken. Here he is no longer seen rolling on the floor, but sitting up, with faint marks of intelligence beginning to beam in his face. After this he was taught, day by day, to pick up a little wooden pin and place it in a hole in a black-board. This was a still greater thing for him to do. In this way his patient teachers led him on step by step. When he had been in the institution three years the third picture was taken. It represents him as intelligent, and pleasing in face and form, with nothing to show that he had ever been an idiot. His mind is restored, and he is reading a book. Not only this, but he has been taught 'the old, old story of Jesus and His love.' He gives good evidence of being a Christian. And the idiot who not long since used to rest upon and roll about the floor, and seemed to have no more mind than a stock or a stone, is now looking up to heaven, and hoping by and by to be 'equal with the angels.' I think this is a good illustration of the meaning of our text. Here indeed we seem to see 'patience having her *perfect* work.' Such an example as this should help us to learn the lesson of patience perfectly.

But we must look away from these to God our Saviour for the best example of patience.

Think how He creates and preserves us, and bestows unnumbered mercies and blessings upon us; yet how often we forget Him, and refuse to do what He tells us, and go on doing the very thing that He hates. Think how patient He is, and how He still continues to watch over, and love, and shower down His benefits upon us; and then we see how wonderful God's patience is. The Jews tell a good story about Abraham that illustrates this point of our subject very clearly.

The story says that one day Abraham was sitting at the door of his tent, according to his custom, and watching for strangers passing by, that he might entertain them. As he thus watched he saw an old man coming towards him. He was an hundred years old, and leaned on his staff, bowed down with the weight of years and infirmities. He moved slowly on. Abraham invited him into his tent; he received him kindly, and bade him rest. Abraham washed the old man's feet, and had a nice supper prepared

THE LESSON OF PATIENCE.

for him; but he was surprised to see the stranger begin his meal without waiting to ask God's blessing. Abraham asked him why he did not worship the God of heaven. The old man said that he worshipped fire only, and did not acknowledge any other god.

This made Abraham angry. He thrust the old man out of his tent, without food or shelter for the night. When the old man was gone, God called to Abraham, and asked him where the stranger was. Abraham answered: 'I thrust him out of my tent, Lord, because he refused to worship Thee.'

'I have borne with him,' said the Lord, 'for an hundred years, though he denied and disobeyed me. Couldest thou not bear with him for one night?' Abraham sought the old man, and brought him back. He gave him food and shelter, and taught him to know the true God.

Thus Abraham learned the lesson of patience, as we should do, from the example God sets in the way in which He bears with us.

How patient Jesus was all the days of His life on earth! 'When He was reviled, He reviled not again; when He suffered, He threatened not.' And oh, how wonderfully patient when on trial before His death! His enemies were raging round Him like wild beasts, bringing all sorts of false charges against Him; but He was calm and gentle as a lamb. In the words of Isaiah, 'He was brought as a lamb to the slaughter, and as a sheep before her shearers is dumb, so He opened not His mouth.' And we should learn the lesson of patience because of the help we have in the examples of those who have practised this lesson before us.

But this lesson of patience can be learned only by the help of God's grace. If we ask Him in earnest prayer, He will give us also the help of His grace, and enable us to learn the lesson of patience and practise it. 'Let patience have her perfect work;' this is our text. The lesson of patience; this is our subject. We have spoken of three reasons why we ought to learn this lesson: because of *the comfort it gives;* because of *the good it does;* because of *the help we have* in learning it. Let us look to Jesus, and offer the prayer :

> 'Thy fair example may we trace,
>   To teach us what we ought to be;
> Make us by Thy transforming grace,
>   Dear Saviour, daily more like Thee.'

VI.

'𝔚𝔥𝔞𝔱𝔰𝔬𝔢𝔳𝔢𝔯 𝔱𝔥𝔶 𝔥𝔞𝔫𝔡 𝔣𝔦𝔫𝔡𝔢𝔱𝔥 𝔱𝔬 𝔡𝔬, 𝔡𝔬 𝔦𝔱 𝔴𝔦𝔱𝔥 𝔱𝔥𝔶 𝔪𝔦𝔤𝔥𝔱.'—
ECCLES. ix. 10.

SUPPOSE we see a man who is in the habit of getting up early in the morning to attend to business. He is busy all day without stopping, except to eat his meals, never resting till he goes home at night. Should we call him an idle or an industrious man? An industrious man, of course. We know that he is diligent in business; and this is the lesson which Solomon is teaching us in the words of our text, when he says, 'Whatsoever thy hand findeth to do, do it with thy might.'

Sometimes we see people who are very industrious in many things, and most careless and slothful in others. They are very diligent all the week in attending to the business of this world, but when Sunday comes, careless of the things belonging to God and the soul. They have neither diligence nor industry; they live as if they had no souls. This indifference shows us that we are sinners. Sin is like a disease. It acts upon the soul in just the same way that sickness acts on the body. When well, we love to run about and be active. We need no one to tell us so to do; we do it of ourselves. We take real pleasure in walking, or running, or jumping.

But when we are sick it is altogether different. Our strength is gone; we have no desire to move;

our only wish is to be still. And it is so with our souls. If they were well, or in a healthy state, we would love to read the Bible, and pray, and talk about God, and do everything that would draw us to Him; but the disease of sin is in our souls. This leads us to neglect them. This disease must be healed. The Bible is the tree of life, and 'the leaves of this tree are for the healing of the nations.' In our text Solomon plucks a leaf from this tree. It is a leaf for the cure of idleness. It does this by teaching the lesson of diligence. The subject of our lesson to-day is—*The cure of idleness, or the lesson of diligence.*

And there are three things that God has given us in connection with this lesson of diligence, which show the necessity of learning it.

In the first place, God has given COMMANDS *about diligence, which show its importance.*

If God thinks it worth while to give commands as to diligence, surely it is worth while for us to attend to them. God gives commands about many things. Some are more important than others. The Jews thought that the least of all God's commandments was that about birds' nests. Perhaps you never knew there was such a command in the Bible; but there is. You will find it in the twenty-second chapter of Deuteronomy, sixth verse. Here God says that if we find a bird's nest with eggs or young birds in it, and the old bird sitting on the nest, if we take away the young birds or the eggs, we are not to take the old bird with them. How wonderful it is, that the great God, whose throne is in the heaven, and who governs thousands of worlds, should make a law about so small a thing as a bird's nest! But it only shows how good God is.

This command about birds' nests is not an important one; but when God speaks about more important things, He gives not merely *one* command, but many. The lesson of diligence, of which we are now speaking, is very important. It is important for the body as well as the soul,—it is important for this world as well as for the next; and so God repeats it in the Bible. In looking through the Bible, I found in a short time between thirty and forty different commands that God has given to teach us the lesson of diligence. We find these commands both in the Old Testament and in the New. They are repeated in different words, in order that we may lay them to heart.

God commands diligence about the affairs of this life when He says to us, 'Be thou *diligent* to know the state of thy flocks and of thine herds' (Prov. xxvii. 23). In the times when the Bible was written, the principal property of people was in cattle. This, then, is an Old Testament command to diligence in our worldly affairs. And the Apostle Paul gives us a similar command in the New Testament when he says, 'Be not slothful in business; fervent in spirit; serving the Lord' (Rom. xii. 11). This refers to business of all kinds; and it shows how diligent God desires us to be in all things.

And then God commands us to be diligent about our souls as well as our bodies. This is what He means when He says, 'Keep thine *heart* with all *diligence;* for out of it are the issues of life' (Prov. iv. 23). And this is what He means, too, when He says, 'Give *diligence* to make your calling and election sure' (2 Pet. i. 10)—that is, be diligent in trying to save your souls.

And God bids us use diligence in the words of our text—'Whatsoever thy hand findeth to do, do it with thy might.' This is one of God's commands about diligence. It means that we do all things we have to do in the best and most faithful way.

Let me tell you about a Sunday-school boy, whose name was Abel Baker, how he obeyed this command of God, and the good that came from his obedience.

The Sunday-school that Abel attended was in England. One day the superintendent of the school took the words of our text as the subject of an earnest address. He told the scholars that this was God's command to every one of them, and that God wanted them all to learn the lesson of diligence, and do everything they had to do in the very best way they could. Abel listened attentively to every word the superintendent said. He was a steady little fellow, fond enough of fun in a quiet way, but inclined to be lazy, especially in studying his lessons. While listening to the superintendent, he remembered how often his mother had to scold him for only half doing what he had to do; and he made up his mind that she should no longer have cause to find fault. He thought it would not be so very hard to do this, except in his lessons. He was not a very smart scholar. It took him a long time to learn his lessons, even in the poor way in which he generally said them; and if he should undertake to get them perfectly, he thought he would have no time for play. But still his teacher's words pressed hard upon him. On his way home he repeated the text to himself, to fix it in his memory: 'Whatsoever thy hand findeth to do, do it with thy might.' He thought about this, and said to himself, 'This word "*whatsoever*" is a pretty big word. It takes in lessons as well as play and work. Geography, spelling lessons, sums, and everything must be done in this way. This is pretty hard; but I'll try.'

And he did try. From that day he began to be diligent. He went to work with a will. He studied his lessons, and did everything with all his might. When he left school he was bound apprentice to a blacksmith. He remembered this lesson of diligence still, and practised it too. He swung his hammer vigorously, and made the anvil ring again. All the old laziness which he had when a boy was overcome. He was active, industrious, and diligent; not only in his trade, but in all things. He became a Christian, and joined the church; and he was just as diligent in his religion as he was in his business. He was known to be the best blacksmith in that part of England. He never slighted anything. 'Whatsoever his hand found to do, he did it with his might.' And now see what came of this habit of diligence.

The London Missionary Society had resolved to build a missionary ship. One of the missionaries who was going out in her had been the Sunday-school teacher of Abel Baker. He knew what a good blacksmith he was, and he got him engaged to make one of the anchors and chains for the ship; for he knew it would be well made.

The vessel is finished and furnished. She has started on her way, and has nearly reached the end of her voyage in safety. Then she encounters a fearful storm. The wind is driving her on towards a rocky island in the Pacific Ocean. All on board hear the roar of the breakers. Unless the vessel can be kept from drifting, she will soon be dashed to pieces, and all on board must perish. What is to be done? Above the howling of the storm the captain's voice is heard crying, 'Let go the anchor!' 'Ay, ay! sir,' is the ready answer of the crew. Away goes the anchor to the bottom of the sea. For a moment the vessel stops drifting. But will the anchor be able to hold her? No. A huge wave strikes the ship. A sharp sound is heard; the chain has snapped, and the ship is drifting again towards the breakers. 'Let go another anchor.' It goes, and fails like the first. A third is tried, but with no better success. There is only one more left. This is a smaller one than the others, and the chain is lighter. But it had been carefully made by hand instead of by machinery. They look at it in doubt and fear. It does not seem worth while to try that slender thing when the heavier chains had snapped like thread. 'Try it, try it,' said one of the missionaries. ' My old scholar, Abel Baker, made it; and I know it is made in the best way that a chain can be made.'

Away goes Abel Baker's anchor. It is their last hope. If that fails, then they must perish. How anxiously they watch the result ! The anchor reaches the bottom. It holds. The ship stops drifting. But will it continue to bear the strain upon it ? The vessel rises and falls with the swelling waves. The chain swings backwards and forwards. The anchor holds. The vessel is held steady till the storm is over, and they are saved. The anchor and the chain that Abel Baker made '*with his might*' saved that ship.

And thus we see, my dear children, how much good was done by one scholar remembering this short text. It saved a noble ship, with the lives of those faithful missionaries, and of all on board.

We ought to learn this lesson of diligence, in the first place, because of the *commands* God has given us.

But, in the second place, we should learn this lesson of diligence because of the PROMISES *God has given about it.*

How good of God to give us promises to stir us up to our duty! He was not obliged to do this. He might have given commands, and then have threatened punishment if we did not obey them. But He has not done so. There are indeed threatenings in God's word, which we ought to heed. But then the Bible is filled with great and precious promises; and very

THE LESSON OF DILIGENCE. 85

many of these are promises about diligence. Let us now look at some of them.

In the book of Proverbs, xiii. 4, we read: 'The soul of the sluggard desireth, and hath nothing; but *the soul of the diligent shall be made fat.*' A fat soul means one that is ripening like fruit on a tree, and growing in right, and good, and holy feelings. This is a promise that if we are diligent in reading the Bible, and praying, and attending Sunday-school and church, then God will bless our souls, and make them prosper. There are other promises also: 'He that *diligently* seeketh good, secureth favour' (Prov. xi. 27). 'He that dealeth with a slack hand becometh poor, but *the hand of the diligent maketh rich*' (Prov. x. 4). 'The slothful shall be under tribute, but the *hand of the diligent shall bear rule*' (Prov. xii. 24). 'The *thoughts* of the *diligent* tend only to *plenteousness*' (Prov. xxi. 5). 'Seest thou a man *diligent* in his business? *he shall stand before kings;* he shall not stand before mean men' (Prov. xxii. 29).

But we cannot repeat all the promises that God gives in His word about the blessings He will bestow on those who learn and practise the lesson of diligence. In the world around us, as well as in the Bible, we find illustrations of this grand truth.

There was once a German duke who disguised himself, and during the night placed a large stone in the middle of the road near his palace.

Next morning a sturdy peasant, named Hans, came that way with his lumbering ox-cart. 'Oh, these lazy people!' said he. 'Here is this big stone, right in the middle of the road, and no one will take the trouble to put it out of the way.' And so Hans went on, scolding about the laziness of the people.

Then came a gay soldier along. A bright plume waved from his helmet, and a sword dangled by his side. as he went singing on his way. He held his head so high that he did not see the stone, so he stumbled over it, and fell with his sword between his legs. This stopped his song, and he began to storm at the country people, and called them 'boors and blockheads for leaving a huge stone in the road to break a gentleman's shins on.' So he passed along.

Now came a company of merchants, with pack-horses and goods, on their way to the fair that was to be held at the village near the duke's palace. When they came to the stone, the road was so narrow that they had to go in single file on either side. One of them, named Berthold, cried out:

'Did anybody ever see the like of that big stone, lying here all the morning, and never a soul putting a hand to it?'

It lay there for three weeks, and no one took the trouble to remove it. Then the duke sent word to all the people on his lands to meet at a deep cut in the road, called the Dornthou, near where this rock lay, as he had something to tell them.

The day came, and crowds gathered at the Dornthou. Old Hans the farmer was there, and so was Berthold the merchant. Hans said: 'I hope my lord duke will now find out what a lazy set of people he has under him.'

'Shame on them!' said Berthold. And now a loud horn was heard, and the people stretched their necks and strained their eyes looking towards the castle, as a splendid cavalcade came galloping on to the Dornthou. The duke rode up to the cut, got down from his horse, and, smiling, spoke thus to the people:

'My friends, it was I who put this stone here three weeks ago. Every passer-by has left it just where it was, and has scolded his neighbour for not taking the trouble to remove it.'

When he had spoken these words he stooped down

and lifted up the stone. Underneath was a round hollow, lined with white pebbles, and in it lay a small leathern bag. The duke held up this bag, so that all the people might see what was written on a piece of paper fastened to the bag. These were the words: '*For him who lifts the stone.*'

He untied the bag, turned it upside down, and out of it fell a beautiful gold ring and twenty large bright golden coins.

Then every one wished that he had been diligent enough to move the stone, instead of going round about it, and finding fault with his neighbour. They all lost that prize because they had not learned the lesson or formed the habit of diligence. And WE shall lose many a prize if we do not form this habit. That bag of money was the duke's promise of a reward to diligence. But it was hidden under the stone, so that no one could see it. God's promises to the diligent are not hidden in this way. They are written plainly in the Bible, so that we may all see and understand them.

Dr. Franklin used to say, 'What though you have found no treasure, and had no legacy left you? Never mind! Remember that diligence is the mother of good luck. God gives all things to industry.

" Then plough deep while sluggards sleep,
And you'll have corn to sell and keep."

Work while it is called to-day, for you know not how you may be hindered to-morrow. One to-day is worth two to-morrows; and never leave till to-morrow anything that can be done to-day.'

The second reason why we ought to learn this lesson of diligence is because of the *promises* God has given about it.

The third reason why we ought to learn this lesson is, because of the EXAMPLES *God has given.*

If we look into the Bible, we find many examples of persons who had learned this great lesson of diligence. They practised it, and found God's promises true. Nearly all the good men of whom we read in the Bible were diligently engaged in attending to their business when God called them to work for Him, in the different ways which have made them famous in the world.

There is Moses, for example. He was diligently attending to his flocks in the desert when God appeared to him in the burning bush, and sent him on the great work of delivering His people Israel out of Egypt, and of leading them through the wilderness in such a wonderful way.

There is Gideon, in the time of the judges. He was diligently engaged in threshing wheat when the angel of God came to him, and told him how he was to deliver Israel from their enemies who were oppressing them.

There is David. He was only a boy when Samuel came to anoint him to be king over Israel in the place of Saul; but, boy as he was, he *had* learned the lesson of diligence. He was not playing or idling about, but was industriously employed in taking care of his father's sheep.

When God directed Elijah to appoint Elisha as prophet in his place, he found him diligently engaged in ploughing with twelve yoke of oxen. And when our Saviour made choice of the men who were to be His apostles, and spread the glad tidings of salvation through the earth, some, like Andrew and Peter, were diligently engaged in fishing; and others, as James and John, were mending their nets.

God promised to bless Jacob when he left his father's house and went to live with his uncle Laban. And He did bless him, and made him very rich; but He did not bless him in idleness. Jacob was a pat tern of steady industry and untiring diligence, and it was in this way that the blessing came to him. And it was the same with his son Joseph. Whether he was in the house of Potiphar or in the prison of the captain of the guard, he attended diligently to the duties before him; and it was *this*, through God's blessing, that brought him to stand before Pharaoh as the ruler over the land of Egypt.

And when we look outside of the Bible, how many examples we find of the good that follows the habit of diligence! Let us look at one or two of them.

A few years ago, a gentleman who kept a large drug shop in Boston advertised for a boy. The next day a number of boys applied for the situation. One of them was a queer-looking little fellow. He came with his aunt, who took care of him. Looking at the poor boy, the merchant said promptly, 'Can't take *him;* he's too small.'

'I know he's small,' said his aunt, 'but he's *willing* and *faithful*. Please try him, sir.'

There was something in the boy's look which made the merchant think again. A partner in the firm came forward and said he 'didn't see what they wanted with such a boy—he wasn't bigger than a pint pot.' Still the boy was allowed to stay, and put to work.

Not long after a call was made on the clerks for some one to stay through the night. They all held back but little Charley, who instantly offered his services. In the middle of the night the merchant came to the shop to see if all was right, and was surprised to find Charley busy cutting out labels.

'What are you doing?' he asked. 'I didn't tell you to work all night.'

'I know you didn't, sir; but I thought I had better be doing something than be idle.'

In the morning, when the merchant came into his

office, he said to the cashier, 'Double Charley's wages. His aunt said he was *willing*, and so he is.'

A few weeks after this a menagerie passed through the streets. Naturally enough, all the hands in the shop rushed out to see it, but Charley stayed in his place. A thief saw his chance, and entered by the back door; suddenly he found himself grabbed by the young clerk, and held down to the floor. Not only was he prevented from stealing, but things taken from other shops were found upon him and returned to their owners.

'What made you stay to watch when all the others quitted their work to look?' asked the merchant.

'You told me never to leave the shop, sir, when others were absent, and so I thought I ought to stay.'

The order was repeated, 'Double that boy's wages. His aunt said he was *faithful*, and so he is.'

Before he left the clerkship he was getting a salary of £500 a year; and now he is a member of the firm. Here is an example of diligence leading to success. And no boy or girl, man or woman, will be long out of a place who learns the lesson of diligence, and practises it in this way.

A long time ago there was an old king in Europe, who owned a splendid forest, filled with deer and all kinds of game. At the edge of this forest lived an old peasant, named Cuno, whose duty it was to take care of the forest. He had a son named Hanschen, about sixteen years old. The king was very fond of hunting. He was himself an excellent archer, and he desired to encourage his people in skilful archery.

He gave notice once that on the next New Year's-day he would assemble all the young men in that part of the country under twenty years of age, in the park near his favourite palace, for a trial of skill in shooting, and that the best bowman should receive a valuable prize.

THE LESSON OF DILIGENCE.

Time passed on. New Year's-day came round, and the young men from all parts of the country gathered in the park. The mark was a new gold coin in the centre of the target, that was covered with silver paper. It was placed at the distance of 70 yards, and each archer was to have three shots.

The shooting began very briskly, and went on for a time without any one hitting the mark, though several struck the silver paper. When all the rest had tried without success, the king feared that no one would win the prize. Then old Cuno called for his son Hanschen to try his skill.

Hanschen, plainly dressed in home-spun clothes, and awkward in his movements, because unaccustomed to such fine company, calls forth the merriment of the gentlemen's sons around him. He cares not for this.

He takes up his bow and fits an arrow to it. He carefully draws the string to his ear, and takes a steady aim. The arrow flies through the air. It strikes the mark in the centre, and brings it to the ground. A loud shout of applause bursts from the admiring crowd. Then the king takes from one of his attendants a piece of parchment, and reads as follows :—

'To the person who wins this prize I give the forest in which my faithful old servant Cuno lives.' Thus Hanschen became the owner of that valuable property. And how did he gain it? Not by what we call 'good luck,' but by practising the lesson of diligence.

No sooner did he hear that the king had offered a prize to the best bowman than he began to practise, and he kept on practising all the year. Day by day, and many times a day, he would take his bow and arrows and practise in the forest, shooting at leaves and other marks that he set up. It was simply by the habit of diligence that he won the prize. And the one reason why the other young men lost that prize was, that they had *not* learned the lesson of diligence.

'There, that'll do,' said Harry, throwing down the shoe brush, 'my boots don't shine much. No matter, who cares?'

'Whatever is worth doing is worth doing well,' said a serious but pleasant voice.

Harry started, and turned round to see who spoke. It was his father. Harry blushed. His father said, 'Harry, my boy, your boots look very dull; pick up your brush and make them shine, and then come to me in the library.'

'Yes, pa,' replied Harry, pouting, and taking up his brush in no very good humour; still he brushed away at the dull boots till they shone again. Then he went into the library, and his father said:

'My son, I want to tell you a short story. I once knew a poor boy, whose mother taught him the good old proverb, "Whatever is worth doing is worth doing well." That boy became a servant in a gentleman's family. He remembered his mother's proverb; he was diligent in everything he had to do. His employer was pleased with him, and removed him from the house to his shop. He was diligent there also. When he swept out the shop, he swept it well. When he was sent on an errand, he did it quickly and faithfully. When told to make out a bill or enter an account, it was carefully done. This pleased his employer, and he advanced him step by step until he first became head clerk, then a partner, and now he is a prosperous man, and very anxious that his son Harry should learn the rule which led to his father's success.'

'Why, pa,' said Harry, 'were you a poor boy ever?'

'Yes, my son, so poor that I had to work as a boot

black and waiter for a living; but by doing these things well I soon rose to more important positions. It was learning and practising the lesson of diligence that made me, by God's blessing, a prosperous man.'

Harry never forgot his father's example. It is a good illustration of the meaning of our text, 'Whatsoever thy hand findeth to do, do it with thy might.' Let us all remember this text.

There are three things which show us the importance of learning this lesson of diligence: these are, the *commands*, the *promises*, and the *examples* that God has given us about it. May God write the words of our text on my heart, and on yours, my dear children, and give us all grace to practise the lesson of diligence which they teach!

When Jesus came to save us, how diligent He was! He knew that every step He took was only bringing Him nearer to the dreadful cross to which He was to be nailed, and on which He was to bleed and die; and yet He never hesitated. He went steadily and diligently on till all His work was done and His suffering ended; and now, when He calls on you, my dear children, to do what is only for your own happiness, and to do it in order to show your love for Him, how willing and glad you should be to learn this lesson of diligence, and 'whatsoever your hand findeth to do, to do it with your might!'

VII.

'**God resisteth the proud, but giveth grace to the humble.**'—
JAS. iv. 6.

IN certain parts of India they have a very poisonous serpent, called the cobra-de-capello. It is also called the 'hooded serpent,' because when angry it has the power of raising the skin round its head, so that it looks like a hood. Animals and men when bitten by this serpent generally die, unless something can be found to undo the effect of the poison and heal the bite. In those parts of the country where these serpents are most numerous, there is said to be a little animal which is their mortal enemy. I cannot be sure of the truth of this statement; but whether true or not, it answers for an illustration here. In size this animal is between a weasel and a fox, and seems to share the nature of both. It hates the cobra, flies at it, and fights it whenever it has a chance. It often gets bitten in the fight; and the bite would be sure to kill it if it were not for one thing. In the places where these serpents live, it is said that there grows a particular plant, the leaves of which are a certain cure for the bite of the cobra. And so, when this brave little enemy of the cobra gets bitten in the fight, he runs directly to this plant, and eats some of its leaves. The effect of this is to check the poison, and to cure the bite. As soon as this is done, the persevering enemy of the serpent attacks him again, and never rests till he has killed him.

Now, sin is the serpent with which we have to fight. Its bite is worse than that of the cobra, because it affects the soul, and will cause its death, unless the poison be corrected. The bite of a poisonous serpent will sometimes cause the body to swell, and become larger than it ought to be. And the bite of the serpent sin has just such an effect on the soul. Sin causes it to swell with pride in a most offensive way. But pride is dangerous as well as offensive. Unless it is cured, it will kill us. And thus we come to the Bible again as a tree of life. The leaves of this tree heal all the wounds that the serpent sin has made in our souls. Here in our present text we have one of the leaves that God has given to help us in getting rid of the pride of our hearts, and so to heal this wound of the serpent sin.

Our subject now is—*The cure of pride, of the lesson of humility*. And in order to cure pride, or lead us to try and get rid of it, God shows us many things about it that should make us dislike and strive against it. I wish now to speak of three things about pride, which show us how earnestly we should try to overcome it.

In the first place, pride is a FOOLISH *thing, and for this reason we ought to try and get rid of it.*

It often happens, when we do what is foolish or wrong, that we cannot see the folly or sin of our conduct. But when others do the same things, or things like them, we see at once how foolish and wrong they are.

We read of the petty chief of a tribe in Southern Africa, who is so proud as to believe that he governs the whole world. When he gets up in the morning, he walks out of his hut and says to the sun, ' Good morning ; ' and, pointing with his finger across the heavens, he says, 'That's the way I want you to go to-day.' And when he has finished his breakfast under the shade of a tree, he sends one of his slaves a little way off to blow a conch shell, and give notice to the other kings of the earth that they may take their breakfast now if they like.

We smile at the folly of this poor ignorant savage. But it is pride alone which leads him to do so. We see how foolish this is in him. And yet, when we give way to pride, it will lead us to do things that appear as foolish to the angels as the actions of this poor African do to us.

There is one thing that clearly shows the folly of being proud. God tells us that all the things of which we are proud belong to Him and not to us. This is what St. Paul means when he asks this question, 'What hast thou that thou didst not receive?' (1 Cor. iv. 7). It is most true that everything we have belongs to God.

He gives things, not as you, dear children, say, 'to keep for good,' but only to use for a little while, and then give them back to Him. And how foolish it is to be proud of things that are not really our own, but are only *lent* to us!

Now look for a moment at some of the things that people are generally proud of.

Kings and princes, and persons in high stations, are often proud of the *positions* they hold. If they obtain these places because they are wise and good, it is God who gives them the wisdom and the goodness they have. And if *He* has given these good things, then it is foolish to be proud of them. But if they get these places without being wise or good, then surely it is still more foolish to be proud of them. It is God who appoints us the places that we occupy. The Bible teaches us that 'the Most High God *ruleth* among the children of men,' and that 'He putteth

THE LESSON OF HUMILITY. 97

down one, and setteth up another,' as He pleases. And God does this, not for the glory of the rulers, but for the good of those over whom they rule. And if it be God who 'ordains the powers that be,' is it right, is it wise, to be proud of occupying such positions?

How many persons are proud on account of their *wealth!* This is very foolish; and yet there is nothing perhaps that people are more tempted to be proud of than their money. But even this money is not theirs. It is God's. The Bible tells us how God lays His hand on all the money in the world, and says, 'The *gold is mine, and the silver is mine,* saith the Lord of Hosts' (Hag. ii. 8). God *lends* it to us, that we may use it for Him. He never gives it as our own, to do just what we please with it.

Now suppose a merchant should give twenty pounds to one of his clerks, and send him out to buy certain things, with directions to come back as soon as he got through, and give an account of how the money had been spent. And suppose that clerk should feel proud of what his employer had entrusted to him, and should boast about it to his friends. Would you not think that very foolish? Certainly. And yet, if we feel proud on account of the money we have, this is just what we are doing. This money is not ours, but God's. He has sent us into the world on an errand, to use it for Him, and not for ourselves. When we get through, we must go back to Him and give an account of the way in which we have spent His money. If we have not used it as God has commanded us, we shall be found guilty before Him. How sinful, then, for any of us to be proud of our money!

Some persons are proud of their *beauty,* or good looks. But this is foolish. Suppose our cheeks are fresh and rosy. Who made them so? God. Suppose our eyes are bright and sparkling. Who made them so? God. Suppose we have a fine head of glossy black or brown hair. Who gave it to us? God. Suppose we have a very nicely shaped hand or foot. Did *we* give it form or shape? No; God did it. And if God gives all these things, is it wise for us to be proud of them? No; it is very foolish. God made them, and gave them to us to use for a little while. Will these bodies soon die? Yes. Then where will they be put? In the grave. What then becomes of them? 'They turn again to their dust.' Then is it wise to be proud of these bodies which God made, and which are soon turned to dust? No; it is wicked to be proud.

Another thing that persons are proud of is their *dress*. This is the most foolish of all things to be proud of. Instead of feeling *proud* of our dress, we ought rather to be *ashamed* of it. When God first made Adam and Eve, and put them in the garden, did they have clothes? No. They were pure and innocent then, and did not need clothing. It was *after* they sinned and fell that clothing was needed. Our clothing, then, is the proof that we are sinful, fallen creatures. When proud of our clothing, we are proud of that which is the proof of our shame. The sight of our clothing should make us feel humble rather than proud.

And then, if we but remember where our clothing came from, we shall see how foolish it is to be proud of it. Here is a fable which shows this very clearly.

A little boy and girl were seated on a flowery bank, talking about their dress. 'See,' said the boy, 'what a beautiful new hat I've got, what a fine blue jacket and trousers, and what a nice pair of shoes! It's not every boy that's dressed as fine as I am.'

'Indeed, sir,' said the little girl, 'I think I'm dressed finer than you; for I've a silk hat, and pelisse, and a fine feather in my hat. I know that my dress cost a great deal of money.'

'Not so much as mine,' said the boy, 'I know.'

'Hold your tongue,' said a caterpillar, crawling near the hedge; 'you have neither of you any reason to be proud of your clothes, for they are only *second-hand* clothes after all. They have all been worn by some creature or other, that you think meanly of, before they were worn by you. Why, the silk out of which your hat was made was spun through the mouth of a poor worm like me.'

'There, miss, what do you say to that?' said the boy.

'And the feather,' exclaimed a bird, perched upon a tree above them, 'was stolen from one of our family, or cast off by some of them.'

'What do you say to that, miss?' cried the boy. 'Well, I'm very sure *my* clothes were neither worn by birds nor worms.'

'Perhaps not,' said a sheep that was grazing close by; 'but they were worn on the back of some of my family before they were yours; and as for your hat, I know the beavers supplied the material for that article; and my friends the calves and oxen in yonder field were killed not merely that their flesh might be eaten, but that you might have shoes made out of their skins.' Then the boy hung his head in shame.

And so we see how foolish it is to be proud of our clothes, because they belonged to other creatures, and sometimes very humble ones, before they belonged to us. And this shows how foolish it is to be proud about anything, because we have nothing which we did not receive. The first reason why we ought not to be proud is, because it is *foolish*.

The second reason why we ought not to be proud is, because it is UNPROFITABLE.

When business men are going to engage in anything, we often hear them ask if it will be profitable. The question with them is, 'Will it *pay?*' This is a very wise question to ask; and if we ask it in reference to the subject we are speaking of, we shall find that it does *not* pay to be proud, but it *does* pay to be humble.

In our text the apostle tells us that 'God *resisteth* the proud, but *giveth grace* to the humble.' We *resist* our enemies; and God resists the proud because He regards them as His enemies. Who would wish to be the enemy of God? Do you think it would pay to have *God* for an enemy? No, indeed. But to the humble we are told that God gives *grace*. There is nothing in the world so profitable to us—nothing that is worth so much—nothing that *pays* so well as the grace of God.

We read in another place that God 'filleth the hungry with good things, but the rich He sends empty away.' The 'hungry' here means the humble—those who feel their need of God's blessing, and who desire it, as a hungry man desires food. The 'rich' spoken of here means the proud—those who think they are very wise and good, and do not need anything. They are proud. God rejects them. He sends them away without a blessing; but He gives His blessing to the humble, for He 'fills them with good things.'

Now let us look through the Bible for examples of the way in which God deals with humble men on the one hand, and with proud men on the other.

There is Abraham. He was humble. In praying to God, he says of himself, 'Behold, I am but dust and ashes' (Gen. xviii. 27). He was honoured by being called 'the father of the faithful, and the *friend of God*.' There is Moses. It is said that he was 'the meekest,' or the humblest, 'man on the earth;' and God honoured him by making him the deliverer of His people, and the greatest leader and lawgiver that ever lived. And Job, and Joshua, and Gideon, and David, and Hezekiah, are all examples of humble men who were honoured and blessed of God.

In the New Testament we read of John the Baptist. What a humble man he was! When he saw Jesus coming to him, he felt that he was not worthy to untie His shoe; but Jesus said of him, that 'among all who were born of women, there had been none greater than John the Baptist.'

Let us look now at Jesus Himself. He has given us the most perfect pattern of humility the world ever saw. He humbled Himself to leave heaven and come to our world; He humbled Himself to be born in a stable and cradled in a manger; He humbled Himself to poverty, so that 'though the foxes had holes, and the birds of the air had nests, the Son of man had not where to lay His head.' He humbled Himself to such a degree, that though He was the ruler of ten thousand worlds, He stooped to wash the feet of His disciples. 'He humbled Himself unto death, even the death of the cross;' and, in consequence of this, the apostle tells us that 'God also hath highly exalted Him, and given Him a name which is above every name; that at the name of Jesus every knee should bow, of things in heaven, and things on earth, and things under the earth; and that every tongue should confess that Jesus Christ is Lord, to the glory of God the Father.' The history of Jesus shows us most clearly how God loves, and honours, and blesses the humble.

And now let us come to the Bible again for other examples of the way in which 'God resisteth the proud.' Our mother Eve was tempted to pride, and the result was that she lost the beautiful paradise in which she once lived. Pharaoh was proud, and his pride brought all those dreadful plagues on Egypt, and then caused him and his army to be drowned in the Red Sea. Samson was too proud to mind the advice that God gave him. The consequence was that he lost his wonderful strength; his eyes were put out, and, as a miserable slave, he was forced to grind in a mill for the Philistines. Haman was a proud man, and it was his pride that caused him to be hung on the gallows which he had prepared for his enemy, Mordecai the Jew. Nebuchadnezzar, the king of Babylon, was a proud man; and in consequence of his pride, he became crazy, and was driven out from among men to live with the beasts of the field. King Herod was a proud man. He allowed the foolish people about him to speak of him as a god; and to punish him for this, he was smitten with a dreadful disease, which caused him to be eaten up of worms before he died.

These examples show us how unprofitable pride is. Perhaps some of you are fond of history. Let me give you 'The history of pride in three short chapters.' Chapter I. The *beginning* of pride was in heaven. Chapter II. The *continuance* of pride is on earth. Chapter III. The *end* of pride is in hell. This history shows how unprofitable it is.

We see the same thing all around us. Look at the tops of the mountains. They represent pride. Nothing grows there. See how bare and barren they are! And then look at the quiet, low-lying valleys. They represent humility. And see how beautiful they are in their greenness and fertility! The highest branches of the vine or tree represent pride. You find no fruit on them. The low branches represent humility. These you will find bending down with the load of rich, ripe fruit that hangs upon them.

A farmer went with his son into the wheat field to see if it was ready for the harvest. 'See, father,' said the boy, 'how straight those stems hold up their heads! They must be the best ones. Those that hang down their heads, as if they were ashamed, can't be good for much, I'm sure.'

The farmer plucked a stalk of each kind, and said, 'Look here, foolish child. This stalk that stood up so straight is light-headed, and almost good for nothing; while this that hung its head so modestly is full of the most beautiful grain.'

Here is a story to show how profitable humility is:

A Tartar chief, or khan, as he is called, went hunting one day with a number of his followers. On their way they were met by a dervish—a man in those countries who pretends to be very wise and religious, and lives by begging. He cried out, 'Whoever gives me one hundred pence, to him will I give some excellent advice.' This excited the khan's curiosity, and he asked the dervish what the advice was. 'You shall hear, sire,' said the dervish, 'when I get my hundred pence.'

Then he ordered the money to be given to him. He took the money, and said in a warning voice, as he turned away, '*Never undertake anything without counting the cost.*'

The khan's followers laughed heartily when they heard this advice, and told him they thought he had paid very dear for it.

But he thought otherwise. 'There is nothing new or striking in what the dervish tells us,' said he; 'but it's true, and it's wise; and if we are not too proud to profit by such lessons, we shall find them very useful. I like this advice of the dervish so much that I will put it on the doors of my palace, on the walls of every room, and on every piece of furniture, so that I may not forget it.'

He did so, and it was of great use to him, as you will see. Some time after this another chief formed a plan to kill this khan, and take possession of his throne. To carry out this plan he bribed the physician of the khan to make use of a poisoned lancet the next time he went to bleed him. The time came. He went into the khan's presence to perform the operation. A silver basin was brought in to hold the blood. On the side of this basin was engraved the advice of the dervish: '*Never do anything without counting the cost.*' This had a great effect on the mind of the doctor. He had not counted the cost of what he was going to do. He turned pale, and trembled. He put away the poisoned lancet, and took another. The khan asked him what he changed the lancet for? He said it was because the other was dull. But his manner showed that this was not the reason. The khan sprang to his feet, and drew his sword. He seized the doctor by the throat, and threatened to kill him instantly, unless he confessed everything. Then he told the whole story. And so the khan saved his life, because he was not too proud to take the advice of the dervish.

The second reason why we ought not to be proud is, because it is *unprofitable.*

The third reason why we ought not to be proud is, because it is DANGEROUS.

We learn from the Bible that pride is a great sin; and nothing in the world is so dangerous as sin. And it is because pride is so sinful that we find such words as these in the Bible about it: 'The Lord hateth a *proud* look' (Prov. vi. 17); 'The *proud* in heart are an abomination to the Lord' (Prov. xvi. 5). There is nothing that shows how dangerous pride is more clearly than to remember what it did to some of the angels. The Bible teaches us that Satan, and the evil spirits who are joined with him, were once good angels in heaven. They were holy and happy then; but somehow or other, we know not how, they became proud. And pride was so dangerous to them that it caused them to be thrust out of heaven and cast down to hell.

In Grecian story there is a fable about a man named Dædalus and his son Icarus, which shows the danger of pride.

The fable says that Dædalus made wings for himself and his son, so that they might have the pleasure of flying. When the wings were finished, he fitted them on very carefully with wax. Then they took their flight in the air from the island of Crete. Dædalus was humble-minded, and did not attempt to fly very high. He got on very well, passed safely over the sea, and reached the town of Cumæ in Italy, near Naples, where he built a temple to one of the gods. But Icarus his son was a proud young man. He resolved to fly a great deal higher than his father He went up nearer and nearer towards the sun, till the warmth of its beams melted the wax. Then his wings fell off, and down he fell, head over heels, into the sea. That part of the Mediterranean in which he fell was called the Icarian Sea. It is said to have been so named in memory of that proud young man.

Here is another fable to show the danger of pride.

Two shepherds, Hamet and Raschid, met in their fields in India during a great drought. They and their flocks were ready to perish from want of water. They prayed earnestly for rain. Soon after this they saw a small, strange-looking person coming towards them. It was the Genius of the earth, who belonged to a fairy tribe. In one hand he held a cornucopia or horn of plenty, and in the other the scythe of destruction. When the shepherds saw him they were afraid, and sought to hide themselves. Then he said, ' Come near, my children, do not flee from your best friend. You have prayed for water. I come to answer your prayer. Tell me how much water you would like to have, and you shall have it. Hamet, you speak first.'

Hamet was a humble-minded man. He said, ' O good Genius, if you will pardon my boldness, I ask for a small brook to run through my fields, that will not dry up in summer nor overflow in winter.'

'Thou shalt have it,' replied the Genius. Then with his scythe he smote the earth, and the two shepherds saw a fountain burst forth at their feet, and spread itself into a gentle stream, that went winding beautifully through the grounds of Hamet. Flowers bloomed on its banks and filled the air with fragrance. The trees were covered with fresher verdure, and the shepherds quenched their thirst in the pure water of the brook.

Then the Genius turned towards Raschid, and commanded him to speak. Raschid was a proud man. He always wanted to have things about him different from what other people had. He let his pride direct his prayer, and you will see the danger that followed it.

'I pray you,' said Raschid, ' turn the river Ganges on my land, with all its waters and its fish.'

Suddenly the Genius put on a frowning look, and walked away towards the river. The shepherds looked with uneasiness at what he was doing. In the distance a roaring sound was heard. The Ganges had broken through its banks, and came rushing furiously on towards them. In an instant it swept over all the fields of Raschid. The mighty stream plucked up his trees by the roots, swallowed up his flocks, and swept him away with them. The proud man, who could be satisfied with nothing less than the river Ganges, was devoured by a crocodile, while the humble Hamet lived in peace beside his gently flowing brook.

Here we see how dangerous pride is. The Bible

THE LESSON OF HUMILITY.

tells us that '*pride goeth before destruction*, and a haughty spirit before a fall' (Prov. xvi. 18); and these fables illustrate the truth of what the Bible says. But we need not go to fables for our illustrations; there are plenty of these in real history. Here are two that suit our present subject. One is furnished by an incident that took place in our own country; the other happened in England.

Before the revolutionary war, the colonies of this country belonged to England. At one time during that period there was war here, between the colonies on the one side, and the French and Indians on the other. Where the flourishing city of Pittsburgh now stands there was then nothing but a fort, called Fort Duquesne. This was in danger of being taken, and a small English army was sent over to aid the colonists in keeping it. The command of this army was given to the brave General Braddock. When he set off on his march to Fort Duquesne, our good and great George Washington—then a young man, and only a colonel—went along with General Braddock as one of his aids. He knew the country very well, and was acquainted with the Indian mode of warfare.

The army has marched on safely till they are within a few miles of the end of their journey. Their way lies through the forest. Now they come to a narrow pass, covered thick with woods. Washington advises General Braddock to halt the army and send a party on to examine the pass, and see if there are any Indians in it. But he had not been accustomed to march in that way. He refused to listen to Washington. *He was too proud to take advice.* On go the men into that narrow pass. Suddenly a volley is fired into them. A number fall. Some are killed and others wounded. They halt. They look around. No enemy appears. It is the Indians, hidden behind the trees, who are firing upon them.

Washington advises the General to break up his men, and let them get behind the trees and fight the Indians in their own style. He refuses again to take advice. He orders the men to stand and fight as they were used to do. They fire at random into the woods. They might as well fire into the air. There they stand, a fair mark to their unseen enemy.

The musket balls come in showers. General Braddock is killed. Every officer in the army is killed or wounded except Washington. Two horses are shot under him. Four balls go through his clothes, but he escapes unharmed. At last the men break and run. Washington rallies them, and marches back all that are left of that gallant little army.

Braddock's defeat shows the danger of pride. He lost his own life, and the lives of so many of his men, simply because he was too proud to take advice. What a dangerous thing pride is!

And now for our English illustration. Some years ago an English fleet lay at anchor in the roadstead at Spithead, near Portsmouth. The finest ship in that fleet was the 'Royal George.' She was the admiral's ship, and carried a hundred guns. Just as everything was on board, and she was ready to go to sea, the first lieutenant discovered that the water pipes were out of order. It was not thought necessary to hand her into the dock for repairs, but only to keel her over till the part of her hull where the pipes were was brought above water. Keeling a ship, you know, is making her lean over on one side. A gang of men from the dockyard were sent to help the ship's carpenters. The larboard guns are run out as far as possible. The starboard guns are run over towards the other side. This makes the vessel keel down towards the water on one side, and rise high out of the water on the other side. Now the workmen have

THE LESSON OF HUMILITY.

reached the pipes, and have removed the difficulty from them. Just at this moment a lighter comes alongside laden with rum. The port-holes on the lower side were nearly even with the water before this vessel came near; but when the men began to take in her casks she keeled over more and more. The sea has grown rougher too since morning, and the water is rushing in through the lower deck ports.

The carpenter sees the danger, and runs to tell the second lieutenant that the ship must be righted at once. He is a proud young man. He tells the carpenter to mind his own business and he will mind his.

But the danger increases every instant. The man goes a second time to the officer, and tells him that all will be lost unless the ship is instantly righted. A volley of oaths and curses is all the reward he gets for his pains.

But now the officer begins to see the danger. He orders the drummer to beat to quarters or summon every man to his post. But before the drummer has time to give one tap on the drum, the vessel has keeled over more and more. And now the men are scrambling down the hatchway to put the heavy guns back in their places. But, alas! it is too late, too late! The water is rushing in. She is filling up rapidly, and before help or rescue can be thought of, down goes the 'Royal George,' carrying with her admiral, officers, men,—as well as noblemen, visiting on board,—to the number of a *thousand souls!* That gallant ship was lost, with all on board, *because a young man was too proud to take advice!* See, then, what a dangerous thing pride is!

Let us try to get rid of pride, because it is *foolish*, because it is *unprofitable*, and because it is *dangerous*. We must ask Jesus to help us, if we want to get rid of pride. He is the best teacher of humility. He says to us, 'Learn of me, for I am meek and lowly in heart.' Let each of us go to Him, and say :

' Rest for my soul I long to find ;
Saviour of all, if mine Thou art,
*Give me Thy meek and lowly mind,
And stamp Thine image on my heart.*'

VIII.

'**Having our hearts sprinkled from an evil conscience.**'—
HEB. x. 22.

SUPPOSE that all the people in the place where we live had some disease of the eye; and suppose that in consequence of this disease some were not able to see at all, while none of them were able to see anything clearly. What a sad state of things this would be for the inhabitants of that place! We read of persons in the Bible who were just in this condition. You will find the account of it in 2 Kings vi. It was in the time of the prophet Elisha. You know that a prophet is one who, by God's help, can tell things before they come to pass. In those days the worst enemies that the Israelites had were the Syrians. The king of Syria often sent his army secretly to make a sudden attack on the army of the Israelites. Several times, when he was trying to do this, the prophet Elisha sent word to the king of Israel of the movements of the Syrian army; and so the Syrians were disappointed because they could not surprise their enemies, as they expected to do. The king of Syria was at a loss to account for this. He thought that some one of his officers or counsellors was unfaithful to him, and was sending word to the king of Israel about his secret plans for the movements of his army. But one of his officers told him that he was mistaken in thinking so. 'O king,' said he, '*we* do not betray your secrets; it is the prophet Elisha who knows all your secret plans, and tells them to the king of Israel.'

Then the king of Syria sent a large army to take Elisha prisoner. He was in a little town called Dothan, on the side of a hill, about half a day's journey from the city of Samaria. The army came by night and surrounded the hill, to take him prisoner. In the morning, when Elisha saw this army, he knew what they had come for. Then he asked God to smite them all with blindness—not blindness for ever, but that they might not see anything plainly just then. God *did* this. Then the whole army were groping about like men in the dark. Elisha went and told them to follow him, and he would show them the man they wanted to find; so he led them on till they came to Samaria. He brought them into the city. Then he prayed God to take away this blindness, and restore their sight. Thus their eyes were opened, and they looked around in astonishment to find themselves prisoners in the capital of their enemies, without a single blow having been struck on either side.

Now, if *we* were blind, what a sad thing it would be! And what we should need then, above all things, would be something to take away this disease of our eyes, and heal them.

It is a good thing that we have no such trouble with our bodily eyes; but the soul has an eye as well as the body. There is one word in our text which refers to the eye of the soul—it is the word *conscience*. *Conscience is the eye of the soul.* I mean by this that conscience is the same thing to the soul that the eye is to the body. God has put these eyes in our bodies, that we may see where to go and what to do. And so God has given to our souls that which we call conscience, and which shows us what is right, and what is wrong—what we ought to do, and what we ought not to do.

But the apostle speaks in our text of 'an *evil* conscience.' This means a conscience that has been injured, like a diseased eye, so that we cannot see clearly. We all have such a conscience, because we are all sinners. In our text the apostle points out the way in which the injury done to our consciences may be removed, when he speaks of 'having our hearts sprinkled from an evil conscience.' Here, then, we have a *leaf from the tree of life for the healing of conscience.* Our subject to-day is—*The evil conscience healed.*

And in order properly to understand this subject, there are *three* questions to be asked and answered.

The first question is, What is the USE *of conscience?*

God makes use of conscience for many things. One of these is, *to guide us and keep us from doing wrong.* You know we have reins for our horses to keep them in the way they should go; and our consciences are the reins by which God guides us, and if we only mind the reins, we shall save ourselves from sin and sorrow.

'Why didn't you pocket some of those pears?' said one boy to another. 'There was nobody there to see.'

'Yes, there was, though,' said the other boy. 'There were *two to see*—I was there to see myself, and I never want to see myself do a mean or dishonest thing; *and then God was there to see me.*' This boy was minding the reins. Remember, whenever you are tempted to do anything wrong, there are always '*two to see.*' And this shows us the true meaning of the word conscience. It is made up of two Latin words, '*scio,*' to know, and '*con,*' together. It means knowing together. God and ourselves are the two who know all about everything we do.

There is a story told of a certain prince which gives us a good illustration of the use of conscience. It is said that this prince had a ring given him to wear on his finger. This ring had the strange power of becoming smaller and pinching his finger when he was tempted to do wrong. It was given to be a help in doing what was right; and he was told that as long as he heeded it he would prosper and be happy. At first he was glad to have the ring, and prized it highly; but after awhile he began to feel vexed with it for pinching him so often, and preventing him from doing what he wanted to do.

One day he set his heart on doing what he knew was wrong. The faithful ring warns him of his danger, but he does not mind; it presses him so hard that he gets angry, plucks it off, and throws it aside. And then, like a horse that breaks the reins and runs away, he rushes headlong into danger.

Another thing for which God uses conscience is as a writer, to keep an account of what we do. Conscience is God's scribe or private secretary; it writes down all that we do, or say, or think, or feel.

During the reign of Queen Mary in England, good Bishop Latimer was brought to trial for conscience' sake. In the room in which the trial took place was a curtain, and behind this curtain a man writing. Whenever the bishop answered a question he heard the sound of this man's pen as he wrote down each word that was spoken. The bishop said that the sound of that pen made him very careful to say nothing but what was strictly true. And this shows us how we should act at all times. Conscience, God's secretary, is writing down everything that we do, 'whether it be good, or whether it be evil.' And the book in which this is written is 'the book of God's remembrance,' of which the Bible tells us, and out of which we are to be judged at last.

And then there is *another way in which God makes use of conscience, and that is as a detector, to find out sin after it has been committed.*

You know we have what are called detective police. When a robbery has taken place, or a murder has been committed, the business of these men is to try and find out the guilty ones. And God makes use of conscience as His detective police, to find out those who have sinned secretly. The Bible says, '*Be sure your sin will find you out.*' And God often finds sin out, or causes it to be discovered through the power of conscience. Conscience at times makes those who have done wrong feel so terribly that they are forced to confess their sins.

A boy once stole a half sovereign. No one saw him but God and himself—the two that we spoke of a little while ago. He was not suspected, yet he felt so troubled and ashamed that he had neither rest nor comfort night or day. He said to himself:

'Why, this is dreadful! I can't stand this for all the sovereigns in the Bank of England.'

Then he brought the money back to the person from whom he had stolen it. He confessed his sin, and asked to be forgiven.

After doing this he felt relieved, and was happy again. It was conscience that made this boy so unhappy, and compelled him to come and confess his sin. Conscience found it out.

And even when conscience does *not* lead people freely to confess their sins, as this boy did, it leads to their being found out in some other way. Many years ago, a gentleman who lived in the island of Barbadoes owned a large plantation and a number of slaves. A sum of money was stolen from his office. He believed it had been stolen by one of the slaves, but was at a loss how to find out the thief. The slaves, he knew, were poor ignorant creatures, who had never received Christian instruction. They thought God was a great serpent, that lived in the woods near their plantation, and they stood in great fear of this serpent. So the planter resolved to make use of the power of conscience to find out the thief. Having called his slaves together, he spoke to them thus : 'My boys, the great serpent appeared to me last night, and told me that the person who stole my money would have a parrot's feather grow out of the end of his nose as soon as I snap my fingers three times.' Then he deliberately snapped his fingers, keeping an eye on the men as he did so. Just as he gave the third snap he saw one of the men put his hand to his nose to feel if the feather was coming. He charged him with being the thief, and found the lost money hidden away in his cabin. It was the power of conscience in that poor slave which made him feel for the feather.

And so we have answered the first question, What is the use of conscience? We have seen that God uses it as a guide to keep us from doing wrong, as a writer or secretary to keep an account of what we do, and as a detector to find out sin when it has been committed.

The second question to be asked is, How may conscience be INJURED?

The apostle speaks in our text of 'an *evil* conscience,' and in other places in the Bible we read of 'a *good* conscience.' An 'evil conscience' is one that has been injured or diseased. There are two ways in which conscience may be injured. One is *by not giving it good light.*

We have compared conscience to the eye of the soul. We may also compare it to the *window* of the soul. A window is of use for letting light into a room, and also for looking through, that we may see what is outside of the window. But if we wish to

HEALING THE EVIL CONSCIENCE. 117

have a correct view of the things that we are looking at through a window, what sort of glass is it necessary to have in the window? Clear glass. Suppose that the glass in the window, instead of being clear, is stained glass—one pane red, another blue, another yellow, and another green. When we look through the red glass, what colour will the things be that we are looking at? Red. And so, when we look through the blue glass all things will be blue, they will be yellow when we look through the yellow glass, and green when we look through the green glass.

But suppose we have thick, heavy shutters to the window, and keep them closed. Can we see anything through the window then? No. And can we see anything in the room when the shutters are closed? No; it will be dark. And conscience is like a window in this respect. We must keep the shutters open and the windows clean, so that plenty of pure light can get in, if we wish to see things plainly. God's blessed word, the Bible, gives us exactly the kind of light we need in order to have a good conscience.

The Apostle Paul is a good illustration of this part of our subject. Before he became a Christian he used to persecute the friends and followers of Jesus, and put them to death. And his conscience did not reprove him. He thought he was pleasing God and doing right when he did this. But he had an evil conscience then. It was injured by the want of light. The window of his soul was coloured by the mistakes which he, like other Jews, made about Jesus. Paul looked at Jesus and His followers just as we look at objects through a red or green glass. He thought Jesus was a wicked deceiver, when He was good and true and holy. He thought the very best thing he could do was to persecute the followers of Jesus, when it was the very worst thing he could do. But Paul then had an evil conscience; his conscience needed light. When he was converted he received light. Then he saw what a dreadful mistake he had made; and from that time he loved Jesus with all his heart, and served Him with all his might.

And many persons injure their consciences just as Paul did, by not letting them have clear light.

A woman forgot to send home her work on Saturday. When Sunday morning came she told a little girl who lived with her to put on her things and take the bundle. The little girl said it would be wrong to do this on Sunday.

'Put the bundle under the shawl,' said the woman, 'and nobody will see it.'

'But isn't it Sunday under the shawl?' asked the child.

The difference between this woman and the child was, that the woman was injuring her conscience by not letting in that light in which the good child saw so clearly.

If we have to go out after night along a dangerous road, full of holes and pits, we shall be sure to fall and hurt ourselves unless we have a good lantern to light us and show the way. In going through this world our path is a dangerous path, and it is very dark too. The Bible is the only safe light to guide us. David is speaking of this when he says: '*Thy word is a lamp unto my feet, and a light to my path.*' We are sure to get astray unless we have this light, and make good use of it.

Let us be careful that we do not injure our consciences by not letting in this light.

And there is another way in which we may injure our consciences, and that is *by not minding what they say.*

The Apostle Paul speaks in one place of men's consciences, which, he says, have been '*seared with*

HEALING THE EVIL CONSCIENCE. 119

a hot iron' (1 Tim. iv. 2). He means by this to show how such men have injured their consciences by not listening to their warning voice.

Notice how thin and tender is the skin on your hand or face. It is so delicate that it can feel the slightest touch. Not even a feather can rest upon it without your feeling it. But suppose you should have a red-hot iron applied to your hand. It would burn the skin off, and make a sore which would give you great pain. Afterwards it would heal over, and the skin would grow again, but the new skin would be very different from that on your hand now. Instead of being smooth and tender like this, it would be rough and hard, and have very little feeling. And the apostle means to say that if we do not mind what our consciences tell us, we shall injure them just as the skin of our hand is injured by being 'seared with a hot iron.'

You know what an alarum-clock is. It is a kind of clock made not to keep time all day, like other clocks, but to wake persons at a particular hour by making a loud noise. Suppose you have one of these clocks, and you wish it to awaken you so that you can rise every morning at four o'clock. You wind it up at night and set the index-finger on the dial-plate pointing to four. Then you place it on a table near the bed, or on the mantelpiece, and go to sleep. The clock keeps on through the night, ticking away, till four o'clock in the morning. Then it begins to strike and ring, and makes such a racket as is sure to wake any ordinary sleeper. This is a very convenient way of being roused from sleep. Yes, it is a sure way, *if you only mind the clock, and get up when it calls you.* But if you turn over and go to sleep again, for two or three mornings, the alarum-clock will lose its power, or rather you will lose your power of hearing it or of being awakened by it. No change will take place in the clock, but a great change will take place in you. The clock will continue to sound the alarm at the proper hour, and it will make as much noise as ever it did, but it will lose its effect. You will sleep quietly on, just as though the alarm had never been given.

Now, conscience is God's alarum-clock. God has wound it up so that it may warn us whenever we are tempted to do that which is wrong. It gives the alarm; it seems to say: 'Take care. God sees you. Stop!' How important it is to have a conscience that will always warn us of the danger of sin! But if we desire such a conscience, we must be willing to listen to it. If we stop when *it* says 'stop,' if we do what it tells us to do, then we shall always hear it; but if we get into the habit of not heeding its warning, and not doing what it tells us to do, then by and by we shall cease to hear it. Our conscience will sleep, its voice of warning will be hushed, and we shall then be like a vessel at sea that has no compass to point out the right way, and no rudder to keep it in that way.

In going along a certain street I sometimes stop at the window of the National Sunday-school Union to look at an engraving there. It represents a grandmother, who has fallen asleep in her chair, with her work-table before her. Her little grandson has crept softly up to the table, and is putting his hand in the drawer to steal a penny. In looking at that picture, I think of a story I once read of a man who was hung for murder. (In a speech which he made just before he was hung, he said that 'the first step he ever took towards the gallows was stealing a penny from his grandmother's drawer while she was asleep.') And as I look at this picture, I think: Ah, how little that boy thinks *he* may now be taking his first step towards the gallows! Conscience is giving him the alarm. It is telling him that he is doing wrong. But if he does not mind what it says, he will soon be stealing not pennies only, but shillings by the hundred, without any fear or feeling. And thus he is in danger of becoming a robber and a murderer, and of ending his days on the gallows.

Remember there are two ways in which we may injure our consciences: one is *by not giving them light;* the other is *by not minding them.*

But there is a third question to be asked about conscience. We have spoken of the *use* of conscience, and the *injury* of conscience. We have all injured our consciences, because we have all sinned. *Then the third question is most important for us to understand. It is this: How may an evil conscience be* HEALED?

The answer to this question will depend upon the way in which we injure our consciences. We may injure them *by doing wrong to those about us,* or *by sinning against God.* And this must be taken into account in saying how the injured conscience can be healed. Suppose we feel distressed in our consciences on account of some wrong done to a friend or neighbour; then the way to get rid of this trouble, and heal our injured conscience, is to go and tell that friend of the fault,—to say that we are sorry for it, and ask his forgiveness, thus making up for the wrong we have done.

Several boys were playing at ball in the street. One of them, without intending, threw the ball against the large glass window of a fine shop. It made a great crash. Quick as a flash the rest of the boys ran away; but the boy who threw the ball stood still. His conscience told him that he had done wrong, but he would not run away. Presently the owner of the shop came out, feeling very angry.

'Where's the rascal who broke my window?' said he.

'I did it, sir; but I didn't intend to do it,' said the boy. 'I'm very sorry. I would gladly pay for it, if I could; but I have no money. Father is dead, and my mother is very poor. But, sir, I'll gladly do anything I can to help to pay for it. If you'll let me, sir, I'll come round every time it snows this winter and clear off your pavement, towards paying for the glass.'

The shopkeeper was so pleased with the manly spirit of this boy that he accepted his offer, and said no more about the broken window.

And the boy's promise was faithfully kept. Every time there was a fall of snow through the winter he was on hand with shovel and broom to clear away the snow. And it ended in his getting an excellent situation, in which he did well.

Now this boy took the right way to heal a troubled conscience. He confessed the wrong he had done, he asked pardon, and he did what he could to make amends.

Let me give you another story of a boy who injured his conscience by doing wrong, and how he got relief from the trouble he was in.

A boy named Charles Harris, in a country town in England, had a counterfeit shilling given him one day by his cousin Thomas Downs, who was a clerk in a store. It looked so much like a good shilling, that scarcely one person in a hundred would have noticed that it was not a good one. In coming home from school the next day, Charley showed the shilling to some of his companions. They asked him why he didn't pass it? He said he wouldn't do that, because it wasn't right. The boys laughed at this, and asked him to come to old Dame Jones's little shop at the corner of the lane, and spend the shilling in nuts and candy. 'You may be sure the dame will never notice it,' said Harry Morgan, the biggest boy in the company, 'for she can't see very well; and then you can treat us all round, and that will be jolly.'

Charley's conscience told him that this would be very wrong, and he said he couldn't do it. But the boys got round him, and coaxed him so much that at last he yielded to the temptation. His conscience gave the alarm when he reached the shop. He drew back; but the boys urged him on. So he went in and passed the counterfeit for a good shilling. The boys thought it was real fun. They enjoyed the treat. But it was no fun to Charley. He could think of nothing but the mean, wicked thing he had done. When he went to bed at night he could not sleep. Conscience put a thorn in his pillow, and there was no sleep for Charley.

The next day in going to school he met Harry Morgan, who asked him to do his sums for him. 'I can't stop now,' said Charley.

'But you've *got* to,' cried Harry. 'If you don't, I'll tell on you for passing counterfeit money, and then you'll have to go to jail.'

Poor Charley was terribly frightened. How he wished he had never seen that counterfeit shilling! He felt that it was very hard for the boys, who had tempted him to do wrong, now to turn against him in this way. But he saw he was in their power, because he had done wrong.

During recess there was a quarrel among the boys. One of them was angry with Charley, and said, 'Pooh! a fellow that would cheat a poor old woman will do anything.' This was almost too much for Charley to bear. But what could he do?

On his way home in the afternoon he met his cousin Thomas Downs, who had given him the shilling. 'Halloa, Charley,' said Thomas, 'let's see that shilling I gave you.'

'Haven't got it,' said Charley, turning quickly away.

'Stop; did you lose it, or give it away?'

'No,' said Charley.

'Well, where is it? You haven't passed it, have you?'

It was on the end of his tongue to say 'No;' but conscience had thus far kept him from lying, and, great as the temptation was, he would not begin now.

'Oh,' he cried, overcome with grief and shame, 'why did you give me that counterfeit piece? It has been a dreadful temptation to me. I have passed it, and what shall I do?' The poor boy looked as wretched as he felt. His cousin was surprised and sorry. He took him gently by the hand, and walked down a lane where they could talk by themselves. Charley told his cousin all about it, and asked what he was to do. Thomas answered there was but one thing to do, and that was to carry a real shilling to the old woman in place of the counterfeit one, and confess what he had done.

'Couldn't I go and put it under the shop door?' said Charley. 'It will be just the same to her; she'll get it, and not lose by the counterfeit.'

'Just as well for her,' said his cousin, 'but not as well for you, Charley. You know you have done wrong. If you are really sorry, make clean work of it. Here, go like a man; be honest about it. You have injured your conscience by doing wrong; you must heal it by doing right. Now, take this shilling. I give it you for my share in your trouble. It will teach me a lesson about putting temptation in the way of the young. Go to the woman and own everything. Ask her to forgive you, and give her the good shilling in place of the bad one.'

Charley did so. When he got the counterfeit

shilling, he went down to the shore and threw it into the sea. Then he felt a great load lifted from his conscience, and said, 'Thank God, I'm free again ! I am not afraid of anybody now.'

And this shows us how we are to get relief from trouble when we have injured our consciences by doing wrong to others.

But if our consciences are troubled *on account of our sins against God*, then how are they to be healed? How are we to get rid of this trouble? Oh, it is dreadful to feel that God is angry with us ! When we know that this is the case, we never can be happy till our sins are pardoned and our consciences are healed ; and it is for this reason that the Bible tells us of Jesus as '*the Lamb of God that taketh away the sins of the world.*' He shed His precious blood, and died for us, on purpose that our sins may be pardoned, and we may be at peace with God. And this is what the apostle refers to in the text when he speaks of '*having our hearts sprinkled from an evil conscience.*'

When the Jews kept the Passover in Egypt, they were told to take the blood of the lamb which they had sacrificed and sprinkle it on the posts of their doors ; and this was to protect them while the destroying angel passed over to slay all the first-born of the Egyptians. And so, when we repent of our sins, and believe in Jesus as our Saviour, it is as though His blood were sprinkled on our souls. We are pardoned. We are safe. That blood cleanses from all sin. It takes away our fear on account of sin, and thus it gives us a good conscience.

A minister was once preaching from the words, 'Be sure your sin will find you out.' In the course of his sermon he said, 'If you do not find out your sin, and bring it to Jesus to get it pardoned and washed away through His blood, be sure your sin will find you out, and bring you to the judgment-seat, to be condemned and sent away by the Judge into everlasting punishment.'

A little girl who had told her mother a lie before she came to church was listening, and she thought, 'Oh that lie! I must either find it out and bring it to Jesus, or it will find me out at the great day.'

She was greatly alarmed, and felt very anxious about her soul. She could think of nothing else, and could not rest till she came to the minister and told him how she felt and what she feared. She ended by saying, 'Oh, sir, what shall I do with my sins?'

'Lay them on the Lamb of God, and He will take them away. Let us lay them on Him now,' said the good pastor. Then he kneeled down with her, and asked God to have mercy upon her, and pardon her sins for Jesus' sake. After the prayer he spoke to her about the tender love of Jesus for His little ones.

The next time the minister saw her she came to him with a bright and happy face. He laid his hand on her and said, 'Well, my child, have you laid your sins on Jesus?'

'Oh yes, sir,' she said, 'and He has taken them all away. I feel so happy now!'

That dear child had her 'heart sprinkled from an evil conscience.' Her conscience had been injured by sin, and the injury had been healed by the blood of Jesus.

And thus we have tried to answer the three questions about conscience:—First, What is the use of conscience? second, How may conscience be injured? and, third, How may an injured conscience be healed? Or, to make it shorter still, we may hang the whole lesson on three words, viz. the *use*, the *injury*, and the *healing* of conscience.

Let us all try to have our consciences made good by being sprinkled with the blood of Jesus, or by repenting of our sins, and believing in Jesus; and then let us try to keep them good by doing God's will, and seeking to please Him in all things. Then we shall be useful and happy, and God's blessing will follow us all our days.

IX.

'Blessed are the peace-makers: for they shall be called the children of God.'—MATT. v. 9.

PEACE! what a beautiful word! How sweetly it sounds! Peace! Peace! And how sweet the blessing which this word represents! When persons have been quarrelling, how pleasant it is to have the quarrel made up, and to be at peace once more! And when war has been raging through a country, filling it with alarm and terror, with cities burned, and fields desolated, and people slaughtered, how sweet it is to have men cease killing each other, and again live together in quietness, peace, and love!

Peace was one of the blessed words spoken by the angel when he came down from heaven to tell the shepherds of Bethlehem about the birth of Jesus our Saviour. He delivered his message to them, and then the angel choir that came with him were heard singing, 'Glory to God in the highest, and on earth *peace*, good-will towards men.' And this was one of the sweet words which Jesus spoke to His disciples before He was taken away from them. He said, '*Peace* I leave with you; my peace I give unto you.' One of the names given to Jesus by the prophet Isaiah was '*the Prince of Peace*' (chap. ix. 6). The kingdom promised to Him is called a '*kingdom of peace*' (Rom. xiv. 17). The gospel of Jesus is called '*the gospel of peace*' (Rom. x. 15). And the ministers

THE LEAF FOR CURING QUARRELS.

of the gospel go on their way '*preaching peace*' (Acts x. 36). And the whole aim of the gospel is to teach men to be at peace, to love peace, and to *make* peace ; and here in our text Jesus tells us of the happiness of those who do so.

'*Blessed are the peace-makers, for they shall be called the children of God.*'

Our subject to-day is—*The lesson of peace; or the leaf from the tree of life to cure quarrelling.*

And to help us to learn this lesson, I wish to speak of three things in which we may see the blessedness of peace-makers. *They are blessed, in the first place,* IN THE EXAMPLE THEY FOLLOW.

It is a great blessing to have a good example always before us.

There was a Polish prince once who had been favoured with an excellent father, and who always carried a picture of him in his bosom ; and when he was tempted to do anything wrong, he would take it out and look at it, and then say to himself, ' Let me not do anything unworthy of so good a father.'

And we should think of Jesus in the same way in which this prince thought of his father. We should look up to Him, and say,—

> ' Be *Thou* our pattern ; makes us bear
> More of Thy gracious image here ;
> Then God, the Judge, shall own our name,
> Among the followers of the Lamb.'

There was a great man in America some years ago, known as General Jackson. He was a brave soldier, and was twice elected President of the United States. He was not a Christian while engaged in public life. But when he retired to private life, and had time for serious thought, he turned in penitence and faith to Jesus, and became an humble and devout Christian. One day an old Kentucky soldier, who had fought under the General at New Orleans, and knew he was not a Christian in his fighting days, had come to visit his old commander at his home, called 'The Hermitage.' He attended church with the General. It was Communion Sunday. And when this soldier saw the aged warrior go up to the chancel, reverently kneel down and profess his faith in Jesus, it touched his heart. He was taken by surprise. When the service was over he was unusually silent and thoughtful. On being asked the cause, he told his companions what he had seen in church, and finished his account in these words: 'I tell you, boys, when I saw that man, who has fought armies, and parties, and cabinets, and who never fought without conquering, get down on his knees in church before all the congregation, I said to myself, when General Jackson kneels in that way, I think it's about time for one to knock under.'

Four weeks after that honest soldier joined the church,—brought to Jesus, and made a Christian, by God's blessing on the silent example of his old commander. It is a great thing to have a good example to follow.

But *we* have a better example than that of General Jackson in seeking to be peace-makers. Jesus is our example. He is the *Great Peace-maker*. He came from heaven, lived in poverty, endured great suffering, and died the cruel death of the cross, that He might make peace between God and men.

When we think of all that Jesus did for us, should it not make us willing and eager to follow His example?

WHAT JESUS DID FOR US.

For us He left His home on high;
For us to earth He came to die;
For us He slumbered in a manger;
For us to Egypt fled a stranger;
For us He dwelt with fishermen;
For us He slept in cave and glen;

> For us abuse He meekly bore ;
> For us a crown of thorns He wore ;
> For us He braved Gethsemane ;
> For us He hung upon the tree ;
> For us His final feast was made ;
> For us by Judas was betrayed ;
> For us by Peter was denied ;
> For us by Pilate crucified ;
> For us His precious blood was shed ;
> For us He slept among the dead ;
> For us He rose with might at last ;
> For us beyond the skies He passed ;
> For us He came at God's command ;
> For us He sits at God's right hand.

The story is told of one in old times, who, when asked what he was, answered, 'I am a Christian.' What are your thoughts, words, and deeds? He answered, 'Christian.' He was earnestly trying to follow the example of Christ. And this is what Paul meant when he said, 'For me *to live is Christ.*' He wished to set before him the example of Christ, and to follow it in all things. This is what it means to be a Christian. And if we are sincere in trying to do this, we shall certainly be good peace-makers.

The thought of Christ's love will lead us to do what we never would be willing to do from any other motive. Here is a beautiful illustration of the power of this love.

A minister in one of our large cities had a gentleman in his congregation in whom he felt a great interest, earnestly desiring that he should become a Christian; for he had no love for the Bible, and was inclined to infidelity.

On one occasion the good pastor prepared a sermon with great care to prove that the Bible is true, and that it is very sinful not to believe *all* that it teaches. He preached this sermon, and hoped that it might incline his friend to give up his infidelity, and love and serve Jesus. He listened to the sermon attentively, yet it failed to convince him, and no good resulted from it.

This gentleman had a daughter, about seven years of age, whom he fondly loved. When he came home from church he saw this dear child's eyes filled with tears, and asked her what caused them. She said it was what her Sabbath-school teacher had told her about Jesus Christ.

'And what did she tell you about Jesus Christ, my dear?' asked her father.

'Why, only think, father,' she said, 'He came down from heaven, *and died for me.*' The tears gushed from her eyes as she said, in her sweet simplicity, 'Oh, father, don't you think I ought to love one who has loved me so much?'

The proud heart of the unbelieving father was deeply moved by this question. What the learned and eloquent sermon of the minister had failed to do was done by the simple question of his darling child. He retired to his chamber. He wept in heartfelt penitence, and uttered the earnest cry, 'God be merciful to me, a sinner!'

In the evening of the same Sabbath he went to church again; but softened and subdued in heart, and changed in thoughts and feeling. He asked his minister to pray for him. And afterwards, when he joined the church, he said, 'I owe my conversion, under God, to my little girl, who first convinced me, by her touching words, that I ought to *love one who has loved me so much.*'

When the minister went home from church he took his sermon and read it over carefully, and then said to himself, and to his family, 'I see there is a great fault in this sermon: *there's not enough about Jesus in it.*' This is the fault of many sermons, and many lessons too: *there's not enough about Jesus in them.* Oh, it is what we tell about Jesus that blesses, and saves, and does good to those who hear us!

A beautiful answer was once given by a little girl

in one of the London Homes for the Destitute. The question was asked why Jesus is called an '*unspeakable gift.*' There was silence for awhile, and then, with trembling voice, this dear child said, ' Because He is *so* precious that no one can tell *all* His preciousness.'

And if we know Jesus as this little girl did, if we love Him, and try to be like Him, we shall *surely* be peace-makers; and we shall know how peace-makers are blessed, in the first place, in the example they follow.

In the second place, peace-makers are blessed IN THE GOOD THEY DO.

No one ever did so much good in our world as Jesus. The Bible tells us that He '*went about doing good.*' This was His occupation,—His daily business. And the way in which He did this was by showing men that God loved them, and by teaching them to love one another. And if we wish to be true Christians, we should try to be like Jesus in this respect. We must learn to love God, and show our love to Him by living in love with our friends and neighbours. When a building is on fire, the best thing we can do is to try and put it out. And when people have angry feelings in their hearts towards each other, it is just like a fire that will burn up all that is kind and good. The longer it burns, the more harm it will do. We are doing great good when we strive to put out the fire of anger by overcoming all unkind feelings. Then we are peace-makers; and we shall be blessed in the good that we do. And this is a thing that the youngest person can do, as well as the oldest.

' I stike 'oo,' cried a little boy, in a sharp tone to his sister, as he doubled up his fist to hit her.

' I tiss 'oo,' said his sister, stretching out her arms, and putting up her rosy lips for a sweet kiss. That dear child was a little peace-maker. She was overcoming evil with good, and putting out the fire of anger in her brother's heart by the gentle influence of love.

'The best way of making peace,' said a good minister once, 'is to *let the innocent forgive the guilty.*'

'*How* do you manage to keep out of quarrels?' said a person once to a good man, known to be a great lover of peace. His answer was a wise one: '*By letting the angry person have the quarrel all to himself.*'

A missionary in Africa was once visiting a man and his wife who were members of his church. Before they became Christians they were always quarrelling; and he asked them how they managed to live so peaceably now. The man answered, 'Sometimes I say a word my wife no like, or my wife talk or do what I no like; but when we want to quarrel, we shake hands together, shut the door, and go to prayer; and then we soon get peace.'

Ah yes, if, when tempted to quarrel, we would only pause and pray, the fire of anger would be put out before it was fairly kindled.

An Eastern prince once asked two of his wisest counsellors to tell him in what way he could do his people the greatest good, and make them the happiest. He gave them two months' time in which to prepare their answers. At the end of that time these wise men appeared before the prince. One of them came bearing on his shoulder a great roll of papyrus leaves, which were used in that country instead of paper. On these he had written out two hundred rules, to show what he thought the prince ought to do to make his people happy. The second came with nothing in his hand, but with a wise thought in his head. The reading of the two hundred rules was very tiresome to the prince. After hearing them, he called upon the other counsellor for his advice. He gave it in two short words: 'Love God.'

'What do you mean?' said the prince. 'I asked you to tell me not what I was to do for God, but what I should do for my people to make them most happy.'

'True,' said the wise man, 'but loving God supremely will secure the highest happiness both to yourself and to your people.'

This was a good answer. It is just what the Bible teaches, when it says, '*Love is the fulfilling of the law.*'

Two shopkeepers in the same city were neighbours. They were both in the same business, and being jealous of each other, they lived in anger and enmity. After a time one of them became a Christian, and joined the church. Then he felt that this state of feeling was wrong. He talked with a member of the church about the matter, and asked him what he thought had better be done in order to make peace with his neighbour.

'I'll tell you what to do,' said his friend. 'Whenever any one comes into your shop and asks for something that you haven't got, tell him he may possibly get it from your neighbour over the way, and advise him to go there for it.'

He did so; one person after another was sent there. The shopkeeper found out, on inquiry, who had sent them; and he was so struck with the kindness of the man he had regarded as his enemy, that he went over to his house, thanked him for his kindness, and with much feeling begged his pardon for all his past unkindness; and from being bitter enemies, they became warm friends. Here we see how much good the peace-maker did.

A thoughtless, bad boy stole all the grapes he could find on the vines of a good lady who lived near his mother. The lady's daughter discovered the thief, and was very angry with him. Her mother said to her, 'Don't give way to such angry feelings, my dear, but carry the few bunches that the little thief has left, with some other nice things, such as she needs, to his poor sick mother.'

She did so; and when the boy saw the kindness shown to his mother by those whom he had injured, his heart smote him. He was so overcome with shame and sorrow that he went to the lady and confessed his sin, and offered her the money he had received for the stolen fruit, and declared that he never would steal again as long as he lived.

The lady declined taking the money, but advised him to go to Sunday school, and put the money in the missionary-box.

He did so, and continued to attend the Sunday school regularly. This ended in his becoming a Christian, and growing up to be an active, useful man.

'Blessed are the peace-makers.' Here we see how blessed this lady was in the good she did to that bad boy.

A good gentleman, whose name was William Ladd, was at one time the president of the American Peace Society. He believed that kindness and love carried out would keep peace between neighbours as well as between nations. But there had been a time when he gave little thought to this matter, and did not understand it. Then, if a man struck him a blow, he believed it was right to strike him back again, without pausing to think if there was not a better way of returning the blow. And if one did him an injury, 'he would give him as good as he gave;' or, as children say, would 'give him tit for tat.' But now he had learned better; and this story shows *how* he learned to be a peace-maker, and the good that came from it.

At this time he lived on a farm, and a poor man, who was his neighbour, neglected to keep up his fence, as he should have done. The consequence was that this man's sheep got into Mr. Ladd's wheat-field, and did a great deal of damage. Mr. Ladd told Sam, his hired man, to go to this neighbour, and tell him he must mend his fences, and keep the sheep at home. But the fences were not mended. The sheep got into Mr. Ladd's field again, and this made him angry.

'Sam,' said he, 'go to that fellow, and tell him if he don't keep his sheep out of my field, I'll have them shot.'

But even this did not do, for the next day the sheep were in again.

'Sam,' said Mr. Ladd, 'take my gun and shoot those sheep.'

'I'd rather not, sir,' said Sam.

'Rather not, Sam! Why, there are but three of them; it's no great job.'

'No, sir; but they are all the man has in the world; and I don't feel as if I would like to shoot a poor man's sheep.'

'Then the poor man ought to take better care of them. I gave him warning; why didn't he mend his fence?'

'Well, sir, I guess it was because you sent him a rough sort of message. It made him mad; and so he wouldn't do it.'

'I considered a few minutes,' said Mr. Ladd, 'and then I told Sam to put the horse in the buggy.'

'Shall I put the gun in too?' asked Sam.

'No,' I answered. I saw a quiet smile on Sam's face, but said nothing. I got into the buggy, and drove off to my neighbour's. He lived a mile away, and I had time to think it all over.

When I drove up to the house, the man was chopping wood. The wood pile was very low. The house looked desolate and forlorn, and my heart was softened.

'Neighbour,' I called out.

The man looked sulky, and did not raise his head.

'Come, come, my neighbour,' I said, 'I have come with friendly feeling to you, and you must meet me half way.'

He saw that I was in earnest, laid down his axe, and came to the waggon.

'Now, neighbour,' said I, 'we have both been wrong; you neglected your fence, and I got angry, and sent you a provoking message. Now let us face about, and do right. I'll forgive you, you forgive me, and let's shake hands over it.'

He did not feel quite like giving me his hand, but he let me take it.

'Now, neighbour,' I said, 'drive your sheep down to my pasture. They shall share with my sheep till next spring; you shall have all they yield, and next summer we shall start fair.'

His hand no longer lay cold and motionless in mine. He gave me a warm, friendly grasp; and his eyes filled with tears as he said:

'I guess you are a Christian, William Ladd, after all.'

And so Mr. Ladd went home, feeling that he had received the blessing promised to the peace-makers. The second way in which peace-makers are blessed is in the good they do.

But there is a third way in which peace-makers are blessed, and this is IN THE HAPPINESS THEY ENJOY.

The happiness we feel in doing good is the best kind of happiness. This is *God's* happiness. The apostle Paul tells us that when Jesus came into our world to bear the cross, and all the shame connected with it, the motive which made Him willing to do it was '*the joy that was set before Him.*' This was the very joy of which we are speaking,—the joy of doing good—the joy of saving souls. And so when we try to do good, by being peace-makers, or in any other way, the happiness that we find is like that which Jesus Himself feels. There can be no joy greater than this. Here is a good story to show how happy a little boy was made by trying to do good in the way of which we are speaking.

One morning, after breakfast, Charley Allen took his little Testament, and opening it at the fifth chapter of Matthew, read some of the rules given by Jesus for the regulation of our lives. He thought they were all good; but the one he liked best was that about 'loving our enemies.' He prayed that God would help him to remember this rule, and try to be kind and gentle when he was provoked.

Then he put away his Testament, and ran out into the garden. This garden was near a fence; and while he was busy in pulling up the weeds, and putting things in nice order, a man passed along the street driving a cart of gravel. He saw Charley in the garden, and feeling disposed to tease him, he threw a handful of gravel at him.

Charley was vexed, but the words came into his mind, 'Love your enemies,' and he quietly brushed away the gravel, and said nothing. After finishing his work in the garden, he went and sat down on the door-step to watch the men who were engaged in building a new house across the way. As he sat here the same man passed again with a load of sand, and seeing Charley sitting there, he threw another handful at him.

Remembering the words, 'Love your enemies, and do good to them that hate you,' Charley ran into the house, and asked his mother for a pear. She gave it to him, and he ran out quickly. Feeling curious to know what he meant to do with it, she went to the window, and saw Charley running after the man, and calling him to stop. The man stopped, and was very much surprised when Charley put a pear in his hand, and then ran off.

The man felt ashamed of himself; and though he often passed Charley after that, he never threw anything more at him. The dear boy had conquered by kindness, and made peace between them.

At dinner-time his father brought him a fine large kite, which Charley had wanted for a long time.

As soon as dinner was over, he went out to fly his kite; but, on trying it, he found that more bobs were needed to steady it. He laid the kite on the doorstep, and ran into the house to get some paper and string to lengthen the tail of the kite. He returned directly, but, to his surprise, the kite was gone. He ran down the street, and round the corner, but could see nothing of it. He went in and told his mother. She pitied him, and tried to comfort him; but it was hard work, and he felt very sorry about it the rest of the day.

The next morning, on his way to school, he saw one of his school-fellows with the missing kite in his hand.

'Why, Joe,' said Charley, 'that's my kite, and I'm so glad to find it.'

'Indeed,' said Joe, 'it's mine, and I shan't give it up.'

Poor Charley looked astonished, and said, 'Why, Joe, my father bought it for me only yesterday, and there's the red line he had put on it.'

'Don't you wish you had it?' said Joe, as he ran off with the kite, too fast for Charley to catch him. The poor fellow trudged along to school feeling very sad, not only that he had lost his kite, but that Joe should be so wicked as first to steal, and then to lie about it.

When he went home to dinner, he told his mother how Joe had treated him. She was very sorry, but urged Charley to try and be patient, and perhaps Joe would bring it back again.

'Well, mother,' said Charley, 'I was very angry with Joe at first, but I remembered the lesson about loving our enemies, and I prayed that I might not feel so; and now I feel that I can love even Joe.' His mother was pleased to find him trying to practise this Bible lesson.

When Charley went to school in the afternoon it was raining, but he had an umbrella, and didn't mind the rain. As he turned the corner of the street, he saw Joe walking before him without an umbrella, and getting very wet. Charley ran up to him, and said, 'Joe, come under my umbrella, for it's raining fast, and you are getting wet.' Joe felt as if he would rather be anywhere else than under Charley's umbrella. But Charley insisted; and Joe had to yield, though feeling greatly ashamed of himself.

After school, as it was still raining, Charley took Joe home under his umbrella.

Next morning, while at breakfast, the door-bell rang, and a fine new kite, larger and handsomer than the lost one, was brought, with a card fastened to it, on which was written, 'To Charley Allen, with the love of his sorrowing friend, Joe.' Charley's eyes fairly danced with joy. 'Mother,' he said, 'I thought the other day that nothing could make me happier than the kite which father bought for me; but I feel ten times happier now.' Charley had conquered himself, and Joe too.

He had been a peace-maker, and he found the blessing promised to such in the happiness that he enjoyed.

Even the dumb animals often set examples that it would be wise for us to follow. I met with a good illustration lately of this duty in a story about two dogs. One of these was a Newfoundland, and the other a bull dog. They belonged to different masters, who occupied warehouses near each other in the harbour of a seaport town. These dogs never met without quarrelling and fighting. They were both very large and very strong. Neither was afraid of the other, and neither would give up to the other. Their fighting never seemed to settle anything. They would fight on till their strength was gone, and then stop only to begin again the first time they met. They were both faithful, excellent dogs, and were highly valued by their masters, who had tried every way to make them quit fighting and be good friends; but they could not succeed in this.

One day these dogs met on the end of the pier that went out into the river between the warehouses of their masters. In a moment they flew at each other in the fiercest manner possible. People tried by blows to separate them, but in vain. They continued biting and tearing each other, and their blood was flowing freely. Rolling, and tumbling, and snarling, and snapping, without knowing where they went, they reached the edge of the pier, and over they plunged into the water.

Water is a good thing to stop a dog-fight. It proved so here. They were more anxious to save their lives than to gain a victory. Each dog let go his hold upon the other, and tried to save himself from drowning. The Newfoundland dog was a capital swimmer, and felt quite at home in the water. He turned his head towards the land, and soon paddled himself safe to shore; but not so with the bull dog. He did not take to the water at all; he was a poor swimmer, and as the tide was running very strong, he found it more than he could do to make his way against it. As soon as the Newfoundland dog reached the shore, he shook his shaggy coat, and then went to the end of the pier to look after his old enemy. He saw the difficulty he had in struggling with the waves, and how he was being carried farther and farther from the shore. Now, a mean, selfish dog, or man or boy, would have been glad to see this, and would have thought, 'Good for you, old fellow; serves you right.' But this dog was a right noble creature. The moment he saw his enemy in danger, all his anger vanished. He pitied him. He plunged back again into the water. He swam up to his foe, took him by the collar that was round his neck, and bore him bravely through the water till he landed him safely on the shore. And what then? Do you think they went to fighting again? Not a bit of it. They were too sensible for that. The bull dog wagged his tail, and went whining up to his preserver, evidently trying to say as well as he could, 'I'm very much obliged to you, my noble friend. You have saved my life, when I didn't deserve it; and now, let's have no more fighting, but be good friends all our days.' And they did become warm friends from that day forward. They were seldom apart after this. They seemed to love each other's society. They performed their duties as watch-dogs in peace, and there was never any more snarling, or snapping, or barking, or fighting between them. That Newfoundland dog was a peace-maker; and even he, though but a dumb animal, found it happier to live in peace with his bull dog neighbour than to be always quarrelling. Peace-makers are blessed in the happiness they enjoy.

And thus we have seen that there are three things in which peace-makers are blessed. They are blessed, first, *in the example they follow;* secondly, *in the good they do;* and, thirdly, *in the happiness they enjoy.* There is no greater blessing than this of making peace. Jesus Himself is the Prince of Peace. Let us try to be peace-makers, and then we shall be like Him.

'*Blessed are the peace-makers: for they shall be called the children of God.*'

X.

'Be thou faithful unto death.'—Rev. ii. 10.

To be faithful means to be honest and true. It means to do what is right, to do our duty; it means we should do this when we are alone as well as when in company; it means that we do it when it is hard and painful just the same as when it is easy and pleasant. A faithful person you can always trust; he is ever the same, behind your back as before your face.

Let us look at some examples of persons who were unfaithful on the one hand, and of those who were faithful on the other, and then we shall better understand what it is to be faithful.

See our first parents in the garden of Eden. Satan came and tempted them to eat of the forbidden fruit. Had they been faithful to God, they would have said at once to Satan, 'No, we cannot do this thing. God told us we must not do it, and we will not.' But they were unfaithful, and did not obey God. How different their lives would have been, and the experience of our world ever since, if they had only been faithful to God!

Consider, next, the brethren of Joseph, when he came to them at Dothan to inquire how they were doing. They first conspired against him to kill him, and then, changing their plans, sold him as a slave to be carried down to Egypt. How faithless were they to their aged father when they tore his darling son so' cruelly away from him! And how unfaithful to their younger brother, when they forced him away, and compelled him to go as a stranger into a strange country!

The Bible gives us examples of a different kind, in order to teach us to be faithful. There is Noah. God told him to build the ark. It took him a hundred and twenty years to build it. The men laughed at him, and the boys made fun of his queer, big boat, without any sails; yet he went steadily on during all those many long years. '*Thus did Noah; according to all that God commanded him, so did he.*' Noah was faithful.

And so was Joseph. When Potiphar's wife tempted him to do what was very wrong, he refused, saying, 'How can I do this great wickedness, and sin against God?' This refusal caused him to be put in prison. But this was better than doing wrong. Joseph was three years in prison, and would rather have been there twice as long than do wrong. Joseph was faithful.

So was Daniel. He was at the head of the great kingdom of Babylon. His duties were many and great. Yet so faithful was he in attending to them, that his worst enemies could find no fault with him, except for his faithfulness to God. He prayed to God three times a day. Daniel's wicked enemies caused the king to pass a law forbidding any one to pray for thirty days. Whoever broke this law was to be cast into the den of lions. Daniel knew this law was passed. He knew that if he went on praying he would be thrown into that den of lions. Yet he never hesitated one moment as to his duty. The Bible tells us that 'he went into his house, and his windows being opened in his chamber towards Jerusalem, he kneeled upon his knees three times a day, and prayed, and gave thanks before his God, as he did aforetime.'

What a faithful man Daniel was! You all know how it ended. Daniel's example is worthy of our imitation. And this is the kind of faithfulness Jesus is speaking of in the text, when He says, 'Be thou faithful unto death.'

This text teaches us *the lesson of faithfulness;* it is a leaf from the tree of life for the cure of unfaithfulness.

And there are *three* things about faithfulness which show how important it is, and how earnestly we should try to learn and practise it.

We ought to learn the lesson of faithfulness, in the first place, because it is SO USEFUL.

Look at a mariner's compass. It is a small, flat piece of steel, called a needle. This is placed on the fine point of a piece of iron, which is fastened in an upright position inside of a little box. It is free to turn in any direction; but God has given that little needle the power of always turning to the north. We do not know what this power in the needle is which makes it turn to the north. People call it *magnetism.* No one can tell what this magnetism is, but we believe in it. The wonderful power of this little needle makes it one of the most useful things in the world. When sailors go to sea, and lose sight of land, this needle is all they have to depend upon to guide them across the trackless ocean. There are hundreds of vessels out at sea now that never could find their way back to port if it were not for the strange power of this needle.

And faithfulness is to us just what the magnetism of that needle is to the compass. It guides us to usefulness. Faithfulness will make us honest and true; it will lead us to do what we know to be right. And then we can always be trusted. Here are some examples of persons who had learned the lesson of faithfulness, and we shall see how useful it made them.

THE LESSON OF FAITHFULNESS.

Mr. Spurgeon gives the following illustration of the meaning of faithfulness. He asked a servant girl who wished to join his church why she thought she was converted. She said, 'I am changed in many things, sir. And there is one thing I never did before: *I always sweep under the mats now.*' This was being faithful.

A good many years ago a battle was fought in Europe between the French and the English. It was the famous battle of Waterloo. The Duke of Wellington commanded the English army, and Napoleon Bonaparte the French. In the arrangements which he made before going into battle, the Duke of Wellington ordered one of his officers, who commanded a large body of men, to take position by a bridge on a road leading off from the field where it was expected the battle would be fought, though some distance from it. He was ordered to occupy that position, and on no account whatsoever to leave it without orders. The officer marched his men there, and held the position assigned him.

The battle began. It was a long and bloody one. The officer at the bridge was too far off to see what was going on, but he was within sound of it. He could hear the roar of cannon and the rattle of musketry, and as the day wore slowly on he felt very restless at the thought of idling there while the rest of the army was fighting bravely. He wished with all his heart that he could join them. The longer he thought of it, the more impatient he became. At last he made up his mind not to stand idle any longer. He called out to his men, 'Forwards—March,' and led them into battle.

At length the English gained the victory. The French were defeated and driven from the field Their only way of retreat was along the road and over the bridge where the Duke of Wellington had stationed the captain and his company. This was just what he had expected. For this very purpose he had ordered the officer with his troops to occupy that position. If he had been faithful to his duty as a soldier, the Duke would not only have defeated the French army, but would have taken them prisoners. This was prevented by the misconduct of one man, who had not learned the lesson of faithfulness.

The Duke was very angry when he found that his orders had been disobeyed. He reproved the officer for what he had done in the presence of the army. The sorrow and shame of the officer were so great that he died of grief. And here we see how useful this man would have been if he had been faithful.

A soldier's widow lived in a little hut near a mountain village in the Austrian Tyrol. Her only child, Hans, was a cripple—a good, kind-hearted boy. He loved his mother fondly, and longed to help her in her poverty; but what could a poor lame boy do, who had not strength enough to join the village boys in their play? When he was fifteen years of age, it made him sad to think that he was a burden to his mother, instead of being a help.

At this time Napoleon Bonaparte, with a French army, was trying to conquer the Tyrolese, and get possession of their country; but they were brave, they loved their country, and resolved to defend it to the last. It was easy to do this if they knew when their enemies were coming, for there were many narrow passes in the mountains, where a few men could keep back a whole army.

An arrangement was made by the inhabitants whereby they could give notice to each other when their enemies were coming. This was by signal fires. At different points through the mountains great heaps of dry materials were piled up, ready to be lighted in a moment; and then the signal fires would leap up till every village and mountain-top would seem to be in a blaze.

The village in which Hans and his mother lived lay right on the road which the French army would take in marching through the mountains, and the people were all busy getting ready for the fight. Hans and his mother had nothing to do but wait.

'Ah, Hans,' she said to him one evening, 'it's well that you are lame, or else they would make a soldier of you, and take you away from *me*.' This made Hans feel very sad. The tears flowed down his cheeks.

'Mother,' said he, 'I'm of no use. Look through our village. Everybody is busy doing something to protect home and country; but I can do nothing. I am useless.'

'My boy, my boy, you are not useless to me.'

'Yes, mother, even to you. I can't work for you; I can't support you in your old age. Why, oh, why was I born?'

'Hush, Hans, my dear; don't talk so,' said his mother. 'You will live to find the truth of our old proverb,—

"God has His plan
For every man."'

Soon after this the Easter holidays came on. The people of the village were all busy with the festival; and fun and frolic and merry games engaged them all except Hans. At the close of Easter-day he offered his evening prayer, in which he asked God, as he was accustomed to do, to make him of some use in the world. Then he went to bed and slept.

At midnight he awoke with the thought in his mind that the French army was coming. He tried to put away the thought, but it would return; so he got up and dressed himself, and at once walked up the mountain path. He kept on till he reached the signal pile. To his surprise, the men who should have been watching by it had left to share in the festivities. Near the pile was an old pine tree. In a hollow place in the trunk of the tree was a tinder-box, and tinder for kindling the pile. As Hans was standing by the old tree, a strange sound fell upon his ear. He listened attentively. Again he heard it. It was the sound of approaching footsteps. He looked steadily in the direction from which the sound came. Presently, by the dim moonlight, he saw soldiers climbing up the cliff. In a second he knew what it meant. The French army was coming, and these soldiers were sent in advance to destroy the signal pile, so that the country could not be aroused. Quick as thought Hans struck a light, kindled the turpentine brand, and threw it blazing upon the pile. Instantly the flame leaped up. The signal was given. Quickly it was answered from mountain-top to mountain-top. Signal fires were blazing everywhere. The people were roused; the French army was driven back; the country was saved.

As Hans, the hero, watched by the burning pile, a retreating soldier fired at him. The shot struck him in the shoulder; it was a severe wound, yet he managed to get back to the village. By this time the villagers all knew who had kindled the signal fire. They gathered round him, crying, 'Hurrah! hurrah for Hans!' They were going to carry him on their shoulders through the village, but when they saw he was wounded they paused in sorrow. 'Carry me to my mother,' he faintly said.

When his mother saw the blood flowing from his wound, she burst into tears. 'Don't cry for me now, dear mother; I die happy. It is true, as you said,—

"God has His plan
For every man,"—

though we didn't know what it was till now.'

THE LESSON OF FAITHFULNESS. 151

Hans died from his wound; but he was happy in dying, for he had saved his country, and provided for his mother, who was well taken care of by the Government for her son's faithfulness to his country.

See how useful he was. Let us think of Hans the cripple, and try to learn the lesson of faithfulness. The first reason why we should learn this lesson is, *because it is so useful.*

The second reason why we should learn this lesson is, because it is SO BEAUTIFUL.

God has given us the power to delight in beautiful things; and in His great goodness, God has filled the world about us with beautiful things, in order that we may find pleasure in looking at them. How beautiful the sky is, as it spreads its great arch of blue above us! How beautiful the clouds are, as they silently float through the sky! How beautiful the sun is, as it rises and sets in floods of golden glories! How beautiful is the moon, as it moves through the heavens so calmly bright! How beautiful the stars are, as they shine in the dark sky! How beautiful the hills and mountains are, as they rise in their grand forms from the earth! How beautiful the trees of the forest are, as they wave their leafy branches in the breeze! How beautiful the fields are, in their robes of living green! And how beautiful the flowers are, in all the loveliness of their varied forms and colours!

We thank God for all these beautiful things, because of the pleasure they give, and the good they do us; and when painters make beautiful pictures, and sculptors chisel out beautiful figures in marble, we thank them too, because we love to look upon the beautiful things they make. It gives us pleasure, and does us good, to see things that are beautiful; and though we cannot all be painters or sculptors, and *make* beautiful things, yet if we try, and ask God to help us, we can all be true Christians, and do beautiful things.

It is a pleasing thing to see a boy or girl, a man or woman, who is trying to be faithful and do what is right. Let me tell you of some boys who were faithful, and you will see how beautiful their conduct was.

Many years ago there was a rebellion in Ireland. In the course of this rebellion dreadful deeds were done, as well as brave and beautiful deeds. It is one of these of which I wish now to speak.

There was a drummer boy, about twelve years old, in one of the English regiments in Ireland. The little fellow was taken prisoner by the rebels, and carried his drum with him. He was brought into a neighbouring town with other prisoners. The rebels ordered him to beat his drum to call their men together; but they knew not the loyal heart that was beating under the king's uniform. The brave little soldier, faithful to his duty, cried out, 'The king's drum should never be beaten for rebels!' As he said this he dashed his foot into the head of the drum, and broke through the parchment, so that his drum never should be used in such service again.

The rebels were very angry, and, instead of praising him for his faithfulness, they rushed upon him with their pikes, and killed him on the spot. Was not this a beautiful example of faithfulness? and should it not teach us a good lesson? We belong to God, just as this young soldier belonged to the king; and if we are only as faithful in using our hearts, and minds, and tongues, and hands, and all we have, for God's glory, as he was in using his drum for the king's honour, what beautiful things we might be doing all the time for the glory of the King of kings!

General Havelock was one of England's best and

bravest soldiers. He was an earnest Christian as well as a brave soldier. Once, while in London, a gentleman called to spend an evening with him, according to a previous invitation. In the course of the conversation, Mrs. Havelock turned to him and said, 'My dear, where is Henry?' referring to her son, whom she had not seen all the afternoon. The General started to his feet.

'Why, poor fellow,' said he, 'I left him on London Bridge at twelve o'clock, and told him to stay there till I came back. Then, in the hurry of business, I forgot it. And, soldier-like, I have not a doubt that he is still there, though it is now past seven o'clock.' The General ordered a cab to be called; and as he turned to go to relieve his son from his long watch on the bridge, he apologized to his friend for his absence, saying, 'You see, sir, the discipline of a soldier's family.'

In about an hour he returned, bringing Henry with him. He found him just where he had left him. The dear boy had never thought of leaving; and if his father had remained till midnight, he would not have left his post.

This is a beautiful example of faithfulness. Let us try to imitate it.

Not long ago, a gentleman, interested in Sunday schools, was crossing the ferry to attend his school in Brooklyn. Near him, on the boat, he noticed a bright-eyed boy with books under his arm, who seemed to be going to school too. He began to talk with the boy, and finally, just to see how he would feel about it, he asked him to take a trip with him to Harlem, a place of great resort for pleasure parties on Sundays.

The boy looked at the gentleman in surprise, and said :

'Sir, did you never read the commandments?'

'Commandments! What are they?' asked the gentleman.

'Well, sir, there is one which says, "Remember the Sabbath-day, to keep it holy."'

'Well, what of that, my boy? Will it not be keeping it holy to go to Harlem?'

'No, sir, that would be breaking the commandment. Excuse me, sir, but I can't go.'

Here the gentleman took out two shillings from his pocket, and, to try him further, said, 'See here, my boy; come along with me, and you shall have this.'

'No, sir; not if it were five pounds. But,' looking up archly into the gentleman's face, he said, 'I should like to have the money, though.'

'What would you do with it?'

'There is to be a missionary collection at our school to-day, and I should like it for that.'

'Well, come with me to Harlem, and then you can have it for next Sunday.'

'No, sir,' said the boy, bringing down his foot with earnestness; 'I cannot go to Harlem. And then I had rather you would keep the two shillings; for I am sure God would not bless money earned by Sabbath-breaking.'

That is a beautiful example of a faithful Sunday school boy.

There was a German shepherd boy, whose name was Gerhardt. He was a real noble fellow, although very poor. One day, as he was watching his flock feeding in a valley on the borders of a forest, a hunter came out of the woods and asked:

'How far is it to the nearest village?'

'Six miles, sir,' said the boy; 'but the road is only a sheep track, and is very easily missed.'

The hunter looked at the crooked track, and then said:

'My lad, I am hungry, tired, and thirsty. I have

lost my companions, and missed my way. Leave your sheep, and show me the road. I will pay you well for your trouble.'

'I cannot leave my sheep, sir,' said Gerhardt; 'they would stray into the forest, and be eaten by the wolves, or stolen by the robbers.'

'Well, what of that?' replied the hunter. 'They are not your sheep. The loss of one or two of them would not be much to your master; and I'll give you more money than you ever earned in a whole year.'

'I cannot go, sir,' said the shepherd very firmly. 'My master pays me for my time, and trusts me with his sheep. If I were to sell you my time, which does not belong to me, and the sheep should get lost, it would be just the same as if I stole them.'

'Well,' said the hunter, 'will you trust your sheep with me while you go to the village and get me some food and drink, and a guide? I will take good care of them for you.'

The boy shook his head. 'The sheep,' said he, 'do not know your voice, and'— Here Gerhardt paused.

'And what? Can't you trust me? Do I look like a dishonest man?' asked the hunter.

'Sir,' said the boy slowly, 'you tried to make me false to my trust, and wanted me to break my word to my master; how do I know that you would keep your word to me?'

The hunter laughed, for he felt that he was fairly cornered. 'I see, my lad,' said he, 'that you are a good faithful boy. I will not forget you. Show me the road, and I will do the best I can.'

Just then a number of persons came out of the forest. The shepherd found, to his surprise, that the hunter with whom he had been talking was the great duke, who owned all the country round, and these were his attendants.

The duke was so pleased with the faithfulness of the shepherd boy that he had him educated, and he became a rich and great man. All these examples show us how beautiful faithfulness is. And the second reason why we ought to learn the lesson of faithfulness is, *because it is so beautiful.*

The third reason why we ought to learn this lesson is, because it is SO HONOURABLE.

The highest honour we can gain is to do that which God and good people approve, and which will lead them to love and think well of us. When we do what pleases them, then we may be sure that we are doing that which is honourable. Jesus tells us that at the last day He will say to each of His people who has tried to serve Him truly, ' *Well done, thou good and faithful servant, enter thou into the joy of thy Lord.*' *That* will be the highest honour that any one can win. And so, when we are doing the things that faithfulness requires of us, we may be sure that we are doing honourable things. Let us look at some examples of persons who were faithful, and we shall see how honourable the things were which they did.

One day there was a debate in the English House of Parliament. A gentleman who had risen from a very humble position was making a speech. A proud nobleman was listening to it. He was not able to answer the gentleman's arguments, and so he thought he would stop him by reminding him of his former poverty.

'Why, sir,' said he in a scornful way, ' I remember when you used to black my father's boots.'

Not at all ashamed of this, the gentleman stood manfully up, and looking sternly into the face of this haughty lord, proudly said, ' True, sir, and *did not I do it well?*'

Ah, that was noble! that was honourable! Faith-

THE LESSON OF FAITHFULNESS. 157

fulness even in blacking boots had led that man up to his honourable position as a member of the House of Parliament. Remember these two lines from one of England's celebrated poets :

> ' Honour and shame from no condition rise ;
> *Act well your part—there* all *true* honour lies.'

There were prizes to be given in a certain school. One of the boys, named Willie, was very anxious to secure a prize. As he was young, the other boys were ahead of him in all his studies except writing, so he made up his mind that he would try for the writing prize with all his might. He did try bravely, so that his copy-book would have done honour to a boy twice his age. When the time came for awarding the prizes, the chairman of the committee held up two copy-books, and said :

'It would be difficult to say which of these two books is the best, but for one copy in Willie's book, which is not only superior to Charles's, but to every other copy in the same book. This copy therefore gains the prize.'

Willie's heart beat high with hope, though not unmixed with fear. Blushing deeply, he said, ' Please, sir, may I see that copy?'

'Certainly,' replied the chairman, looking a little surprised.

Willie glanced at the copy, and then handing it back, said, ' Please, sir, that is not my writing. It was written by an upper class boy, who took my book by mistake one day instead of his own.'

'Oh, oh!' said the chairman, 'that may alter the case.' The two books went back again to the committee, who, after comparing them carefully, gave the prize to Charley.

The boys laughed at Willie. 'What a fool you

were, Willie, to say anything about it!' said one of them.

'I wouldn't have told,' said another.

'Nor I,' said another, laughing. 'The copy was in your book, and you had a right to have the benefit of it.'

Willie heard all they had to say, and then quietly replied: 'It would not have been the truth if I had not told who wrote the copy. I had rather tell the truth, and do right, than gain a dozen prizes. Truth is better than gold.' Noble Willie! That was grand. You see how honourable his faithfulness was.

When the steamer *Atlantic* was lost near Halifax there were about a thousand persons on board, more than half of whom perished; and, so far as we can see, it was all owing to the unfaithfulness of the captain. He was approaching the most dangerous coast in the world. The weather had been cloudy, which prevented him from knowing just where he was. It was a foggy night; and yet he wickedly went to bed and slept when he should have been at his post, carefully watching for the safety of the precious lives committed to his care. The loss of that splendid vessel through the carelessness of the captain will always cover his name with shame and dishonour.

And now let us look at a case the very opposite of this. Some years ago the steamer *Arctic* was lost in the same neighbourhood. She struck another steamer in a fog, and sank in four hours. Three hundred persons went down with her. They were all drowned.

Every steamer has a *signal gun* on board. This is put in charge of a person, who is called the signalman. His important duty, when the vessel is in danger or distress, is to fire this gun, and to *keep on firing* it, so that other vessels may hear, and come to their aid. The gun on board the steamer *Arctic* was in charge ot a young lad, named Stewart Holland. This gun it was his duty to stand by and fire.

As soon as the steamer struck, all was wild uproar and confusion. Every one knew that she must sink, and all tried to find some way of escape. The engineer, the firemen, the helmsman, all deserted their posts; but *Stewart Holland never left his gun.* Women wept, and shrieked, and prayed. Strong men fell down in sudden fear. Some cursed, and swore, and raved; others sat still, pale and motionless as the dead. During all those hours of agony the sound of that signal gun went booming over the waters. The powder gave out. Seizing an axe, he broke open the magazine and got a fresh supply. Again and again the sound of his gun was heard over the deep. But no ship was nigh; no help was near. A number of the passengers lowered the boats, and leapt into them. Others made a raft, and thus tried to escape from the doomed ship.

But Stewart Holland stood at his post. Though all in command might desert, yet *he* meant to be faithful. And, oh ! sad to tell, as the steamer gave a lurch before going down, the faithful gun sent forth its last signal, booming over the sea once more. And as the sea swallowed up the ill-fated vessel, the last thing seen by the survivors was that young hero standing nobly by his gun. He died at his post, 'faithful unto death.'

And when the news of the sad calamity reached us, strong men, with trembling voices, and eyes dimmed by tears, told the story to their children ; and so the name of Stewart Holland became a household word throughout the land. In the words of our text, we see how literally and truly he was '*faithful unto death.*'

It was an honourable thing which his faithfulness

led him to do, and it covers his name with glory. We may never be placed in just such a situation; but from his example, and others of which we have spoken, we should learn the lesson of faithfulness. Let us daily practise it,—at home, at school, or wherever we are. Let us seek to be faithful in little things, and then we shall be faithful in those that are greater. Remember the three things connected with faithfulness which should teach us to learn this lesson. We should do so, because it is *so useful*, because it is *so beautiful*, and because it is *so honourable*. Let us turn the words of the text into a prayer, and ask God to give us grace to be faithful unto death, that we may receive at last the crown of life, which He has promised to those who love Him.

' Be thou faithful unto death.'

' Dare to be right ! dare to be true !
You have a work that none other can do ;
Stand by your conscience, your honour, your faith ;
Stand like a hero, and battle till death.'

THE END.

www.ingramcontent.com/pod-product-compliance
Lightning Source LLC
Chambersburg PA
CBHW022133080426
42734CB00006B/341